KEYS TO INVESTING IN CORPORATE BONDS

Nicholas G. Apostolou, DBA, CPA
Professor
Louisiana State University

Barron's
New York • London • Toronto • Sydney

All inquiries should be addressed to:
Barron's Educational Series, Inc.
250 Wireless Boulevard
Hauppauge, New York 11788

Library of Congress Catalog Card No. 90-35622

International Standard Book No. 0-8120-4386-3

Library of Congress Cataloging in Publication Data

Apostolou, Nicholas G.
  Keys to investing in corporate bonds / Nicholas G. Apostolou.
  p. cm.
  ISBN 0-8120-4386-3
  1. Bonds.   2. Investments.   I. Title.
HG651.A613   1990
332.63'234--dc20   90-35622
                                                     CIP

PRINTED IN THE UNITED STATES OF AMERICA
0123   5500   987654321

TABLE OF CONTENTS

1

INTRODUCTION

Many investors show little interest in or respect for corporate bonds. Even though most corporate bonds provided attractive returns in the 1980s, investors still remember the experience of the 1960s and 1970s, when corporate bonds were actually earning negative returns (that is, total returns were less than the rate of inflation). Other evidence might also have contributed to skepticism about corporate bonds as an investment. In the period from 1926 to 1988, the average total return on common stocks was about 10%, double the 5% return on long-term corporate bonds. Because of the power of compounding, the extra 5% average return from common stock provides dramatically greater profit over time than the average return from long-term corporate bonds. A $1 investment in common stocks at the beginning of 1926 would have accumulated to about $406 by the end of 1988, while a $1 investment in long-term corporate bonds only increased to about $22.

However, this is a case where history may be misleading. Granted, corporate bonds have generally been a poor investment in the past. Nevertheless, investors who ignore this market in the 1990s are missing out on generous returns. Over the past 60 years, bonds have commonly provided less than 5% interest on the face value of the bond. Particularly in the 1970s, this return inadequately compensated investors for the inflation rate. But markets tend to correct themselves over time. Currently, in order to sell bonds, corporations have to price them to compensate investors for the inflation outlook, the greater instability of interest rates, and the consequent increased volatility of bond prices. Thus, many high quality corporate bonds now yield between 9% and 10% interest. As a consequence, a strong case can be made that today's bond prices more than compensate investors for the inflation outlook and the instability of bond prices.

Going further, a strong argument can be made for corporate bonds vis-à-vis common stock. The 9.5% average current return on high-quality corporate bonds compares favorably with the 10% average return from common stock. But remember that stocks are still far riskier than bonds and that there have been extended periods (including most of the 1970s) when it has been difficult to make any money investing in stocks.

In conclusion, if investors want to protect their principal and receive a steady stream of income, bonds rather than stocks may be the answer. Top-rated bonds are particularly interesting for conservatively managed IRAs and other retirement accounts where the interest compounds tax-free. Bond interest will exceed the income to be received from CDs, money market funds, and stocks. Indeed, every portfolio should contain some corporate bonds.

2

CORPORATE BONDS IN BRIEF

Bonds are long-term debt obligations that are secured by specified assets or a promise to pay. In effect, a bond investor has lent money to the bond issuer. In return, the issuer of that bond promises to pay interest and to repay the principal at maturity. A bond's "maturity," or the length of time until the principal is repaid, varies from five to 40 years.

Investors have greater assurance of receiving interest on bonds than of receiving dividends on most common stocks because bondholders are creditors of the issuing corporation. As such, they have a prior claim on earnings and assets, ranking ahead of preferred and common stockholders. Interest must first be paid to the bondholders before dividends can be distributed to stockholders. In case of dissolution or bankruptcy, bondholders have a prior claim on assets over stockholders. Only corporations in extreme financial difficulty will fail to pay the interest on their bonds.

Bond Characteristics. Investment in a corporate bond is the purchase of the corporation's promise to pay interest regularly and to repay the principal at a specified maturity date. Bonds are typically issued in denominations of $1000, called the *face, par,* or *maturity value.* If an investor buys five bonds, the total face value or maturity value is $5000, which means the corporation has pledged to repay $5000 when the bonds mature. In addition, the corporation promises to pay periodic interest at a specified rate on the face value. The interest rate is commonly called the *coupon* or *stated rate,* and payments usually are made semiannually, although the interest rate is generally expressed as an annual rate.

Bond Pricing. The price of a bond is determined by the interest rate stated on the bond, the length of its term to maturity, and the prevailing market interest or yield on the bond. Bonds fluctuate in price, with market value largely determined by changes in interest rates and in the financial rating of the issuing corporation (see Key 10). As the general level of interest rates rises, bond prices go down. Alternatively, as the general level of interest rates declines, bond prices increase. The course of bond prices is largely dependent upon the path of interest rates.

An investor who buys a $1000 10-year bond paying 10% interest will receive annual interest payments of $100. If the market yield for this bond is also 10%, the investor will pay a price of $1000 for this bond. But if the market yield is 12%, or if investors expect to receive a 12% return from bonds with these features, the market price of the bond will decline to $887, reflecting a discount from the face value of $113. At a price of $887, investors will receive a promised yield of 12%. On the other hand, if the general level of interest rates declines and the market yield on this bond falls to 8%, the bond should sell at a price of

4

about $1125. This bond is thus priced at a premium over face value. The key point is that bond prices are primarily a function of prevailing market interest rates, and will fluctuate as interest rates change.

3

TYPES OF CORPORATE BONDS

When corporations borrow money, the interest becomes a cost of doing business. In order to earn money, corporations must take in money at a greater rate than they incur expenses, including interest expense. Borrowing money to generate a greater return than the rate of interest paid out on the loan is called "leverage."

Leverage is a characteristic of corporate debt offerings rather than of Treasury issues. Corporate bonds also differ from government issues in that the ability of the issuers to meet their obligations requires close scrutiny. U.S. Treasury securities receive an AAA bond rating because they are backed by taxing power of the federal government. Corporate bonds need to be secured in ways other than the ability to tax. Bonds differ widely in this respect. A financially strong company may be able to issue a bond that is secured by its general credit. On the other hand, a financially weak issuer will only be able to attract investors if the bonds are secured by tangible assets.

The following types of bonds are available:

1. *Debentures.* The most common type of corporate bond is called a debenture. Investors who purchase debentures are general creditors of the corporation, protected by the overall assets of the enterprise rather than any specific assets. All unpledged corporate assets and property secure debenture bonds. In general, only financially strong corporations with excellent credit are able to sell debentures.

   When a company has more than one bond issue outstanding, the seniority of the issues is often predesignated. A senior issue has a prior claim on interest and repayment of principal over a subordinated bond. This designation becomes significant if serious financial difficulties or bankruptcy threaten the company.

2. *First Mortgage Bonds.* A bond issuer unable to sell debentures or wishing to add additional security to a new bond issue can designate particular corporate property as collateral for the bond issue. If the company defaults on payments due, the bondholders have a claim against the assets pledged. The provision may result in a slightly lower coupon rate for the bond.

3. *Equipment Trust Certificates.* This form of bond is issued by airlines, railroads, and shipping companies to finance the purchase of new equipment. The certificate gives bondholders first right to the transportation equipment in the event that the interest and principal are not paid. These bonds tend to be very safe since the collateral behind these certificates is readily saleable to another transportation company.

4. *Income Bonds.* These bonds are given in exchange for other bonds that have already been issued. These bonds are usually issued only in the case of impending bankruptcy. Interest is payable only if the corporation operates at a profit. These bonds should not be seriously considered by investors.

4

INTEREST RATES

Although bond prices are affected by a number of factors, the general principle is that bond prices tend to increase when interest rates fall, and to decline when interest rates are rising. Given the intimate nature of the relationship between interest rates and bond prices, it is important for investors to understand the nature and determinants of interest rates.

At the most basic level, interest is the price a borrower pays to a lender for the use of money. Interest is usually expressed as an annual rate or percentage rather than as an absolute amount. Thus, if an individual borrows $100 for one year, a payment of $10 on the amount borrowed translates to 10% annual interest. Interest rates are usually set by market forces, but rates vary greatly according to circumstances—most important is the borrower's ability to repay the debt. The primary factors that cause interest rates to vary among bonds include:

1. *Bond ratings.* Bond ratings measure the credit-worthiness of the corporation—its ability to make interest payments and ultimately to repay

the loan. Generally, the higher the rating of a bond, the lower will be its interest rate (bond ratings are discussed in Key 9).

2. *Maturities.* Normally, longer-term bonds have higher yields. Lenders require a higher return to justify forgoing use of money for longer periods of time.

3. *Redemption features.* Most corporate bonds are sold with a "call" feature that allows the issuer to redeem the issue prior to maturity. Companies call in bonds when general interest rates are lower than the coupon rate on the bond since they can now borrow the money at a lower rate. When this happens, bondholders are forced to reinvest the funds at lower interest rates. When an issuer does call a bond, the issuer typically has to pay a premium above par value. As a general rule, the earlier the redemption date, the higher the premium will be.

4. *Stability of the business.* The more stable and secure a corporation's business is, the lower will be the interest rate on its bonds.

5. *Convertible option.* A convertible bond is a bond that can be exchanged into common stock at the discretion of the investor. This provision means that holders of these securities can reap the benefits of rising stock prices. Investors are willing to receive a lower rate of interest in return for the opportunity to participate in the appreciation of the common stock.

6. *Size of issue.* Generally, the smaller the size of a bond's issue, the higher will be its interest rate. Smaller bond issues require a slightly higher coupon rate in order to be successfully sold. This is primarily due to the lack of interest in these issues by institutional investors.

Determination of Interest Rates. Interest rates are set by market forces: The overall level of interest rates depends upon the supply of loanable funds and the demand for those funds. The supply of funds depends upon the savings of individuals, businesses, and government plus the actions of the Federal Reserve and the banking system.

The supply of loanable funds increases as the amount saved by individuals increases. Savings involves foregone consumption. Generally speaking, individuals are more willing to save when interest rates on their savings are relatively high.

The demand for loanable funds arises from three major sources:

1. Households that want loanable funds for the purchases of goods and services
2. Business firms that want loanable funds to make investments
3. Governments that need loanable funds to cover deficits

The demand by individuals for loanable funds is inversely related to interest rates. In theory, the higher the interest rate, the less incentive consumers have to borrow because of the increased interest payments associated with the loan. This is particularly true in the case of home mortgages, where high rates bring higher monthly payments, thus pricing some people out of the market. In considering investments in productive resources, business firms compare the cost of loanable funds with the net revenues to be derived from those funds. The higher the interest rate, the fewer investments exist that will produce net revenues that exceed the cost of loanable funds.

Real Versus Nominal Interest Rates. The *nominal* interest rate is the rate of interest expressed in current dollars. Inflation causes the nominal interest rate to be higher than it would be if there was no inflation. The nominal interest rate rises to reflect the anticipated rate of inflation. The *real* interest rate is obtained by subtracting the anticipated rate of inflation from

11

the nominal rate of interest. If the nominal rate of interest is 10% and the rate of inflation is 10%, the real rate of interest is zero.

Panoply of Interest Rates. Although all interest rates tend to move in the same direction at the same time, an examination of the financial pages reveals there are dozens of different interest rates. The interest rates on corporate bonds change as a result of how certain other closely related interest rates fluctuate. These other rates include:

1. *Federal funds rate.* This is the rate banks pay on reserves they borrow from other banks. A rise in the federal funds rate indicates that more banks are running short of reserves, while a fall indicates the opposite. The federal funds rate also provides an indication of Federal Reserve monetary policy. A rise in the rate signals a more restrictive policy, while a fall indicates a more expansionary policy. However, sharp fluctuations can occur from one day to the next without signaling a change in policy.

2. *Prime rate.* The prime rate is the rate charged by commercial banks to their most creditworthy business customers. Businesses that are less creditworthy are charged a higher interest rate. The prime rate is a bellwether rate: When it is raised, most interest rates will also rise. Alternatively, a reduction in the prime rate signals a general decline in interest rates.

3. *Commercial paper rate.* Commercial paper is unsecured (i.e., no collateral) debt issued by the largest corporations. These firms issue commercial paper because the interest will usually be less than that charged by banks.

4. *Treasury bill rate.* These short-term securities mature in three months, six months, or one year and are issued in minimum denominations of $10,000 with $5000 increments. Treasury bills

are sold at a discount from face value and are redeemed at full face value upon maturity. The discount varies according to prevailing interest rates. Since auctions of the three-month bills occur every Monday, they are easily monitored for new interest rate trends.

5

BUSINESS CYCLES

The term *business cycle* refers to the recurrent ups and downs in the level of economic activity. Although the word *cycle* implies regular, recurring movement, business cycles vary substantially in duration and intensity. Many economists argue that the term *economic fluctuation* is more appropriate for the ups and downs that occur in economic activity. In any case, one of the reasons that knowledge of the rhythm of economic activity is important is its impact on bond prices.

Economists have labels for the different phases of the business cycle. The lowest point during a recession (or depression) is called a trough; the highest point of a boom is called a peak. The periods in between are called expansions or contractions. Expansions have ranged from 10 months to more than 100 months (in the 1960s), while contractions have been of generally shorter duration (7 to 43 months).

Impact on Bond Prices. Trends in economic activity frequently have a different impact on the prices of bonds than they do on the prices of stocks. The direction of stock prices is closely related to swings in the business cycle: In general, changes in stock prices precede major upturns and downturns in the economy. As a result, the stock market is viewed as a leading indicator of the economy. The reason the stock market anticipates economic activity is that it primarily reflects investors' expectations for future corporate earnings.

On the other hand, bond prices reflect more directly investor sentiment about interest rates and inflation. As a result, bond prices tend to run opposite to the business cycle. If expectations for future economic expansion become pessimistic, stock prices will usually decline while bond prices will tend to rise. Why? As the economy contracts, interest rates often decline due to Federal Reserve policy of increasing both the money supply and the availability of credit (see Key 6). Bond prices then rise because they are inversely related to interest rates. When interest rates decline, new bonds are issued with lower interest rates and the prices of older, higher yield bonds rise. This hike in bond prices adjusts all bond yields downward, reflecting current interest rates. After the economy turns upward, and as this expansion matures, interest rates begin to increase because of an increased demand for loans by corporations. This increase in interest rates means a corresponding decline in bond prices. In the last stage of expansion, bond yields are near their peak level. This phase is generally an attractive period to purchase bonds because of the high current yield and the possibility of appreciation in value.

The early phase of a business cycle contraction is another favorable period to purchase bonds. The decline in economic activity means that corporations will reduce their need for borrowed funds. Interest rates are typically at a high level and beginning to decline, resulting in a gradual appreciation of bond prices. The latter phase of a business cycle contraction means the end of the recession is near. Bond prices should continue to rise in response to reduced demand for credit, expectation of low inflation, an expansionary monetary policy, and lower interest rates.

Tracking Business Cycles. The economic statistic used to evaluate business cycles is the trend in the growth of gross national product (total output of goods and services) minus inflation—this is called real national product. Gross national product (GNP) is calculated by the Department of Commerce on a quarterly basis and is widely reported in the financial press. Real GNP has historically grown at about 2.5% a year. When GNP falls below this trend growth rate, the economy is contracting; when it grows above the trend, the economy is expanding. Economists frequently define a recession as a lack of growth of real GNP for two consecutive quarters.

6

FEDERAL RESERVE SYSTEM

Bond prices are most affected by changes in interest rates and thus depend to a great extent on the activities of the organization that has the greatest impact on interest rates, the Federal Reserve. The Fed is the U.S. central bank, and its primary function is the formulation of monetary policy. Although the Fed does not control interest rates, it significantly influences them through its control of the money supply. In addition, the federal funds rate (rate charged for overnight loans between banks), which is set by the Fed, serves as a benchmark for other interest rates. The Fed's actions thus have a vital influence on bond prices; it behooves bondholders to pay close attention to Fed policies.

Structure of the Fed. At the top of the Federal Reserve's organizational structure is the Board of Governors, located in Washington, DC. The primary function of the Board is the formulation of monetary policy. In addition, the Board has broad responsibilities over the activities of national and state-chartered member banks.

The Board's activities are subject to constant media scrutiny because of the influence it has over the course of the economy. The Board consists of seven members appointed by the President of the United States and confirmed by the Senate. All appointments to the Board are for 14-year terms, to some degree insulating the members from short-term political pressures. However, the President designates the chairman and the vice chairman, who each serve for four-year terms; redesignation is possible as long as their terms as Board members have not expired. The chairman of the Board occupies an especially powerful position. The importance of this position is often cited as being second only to that of the President.

Implementation of Monetary Policy. The most important function of the Fed is the control of the nation's money supply. There are three principal tools the Fed can use to regulate the money supply:

1. *Open Market Operations.* These operations control the money supply. They are the most flexible policy instrument and consist of the purchase and sale of government securities on the open market. When the Fed buys these securities, it increases the money supply; when it sells, it drains some cash from the monetary system. These transactions have a direct impact upon bank reserves and are employed continually during the day as needed.

2. *Discount Window.* Discounting occurs when the Fed lends reserves to member banks. The rate of interest the Fed charges is called the discount rate. The rate is altered periodically as market conditions change or to complement open market operations. The discount rate is primarily of interest as an indication of the Federal Reserve's view of the economy and money and credit

demand.

3. *Reserve Requirements.* Banks are required to maintain reserves against the money they loan. When reserve requirements are increased, the amount of deposits supported by the supply of reserves is reduced and banks have to reduce their loans. Although this tool is powerful, it is less flexible than the other two policy instruments and, therefore, is seldom used.

Creation of Money. The money supply is defined as currency in the hands of the public plus transactions accounts in depository institutions and traveler's checks. The Federal Reserve and depository institutions determine the money supply. Currency—cash and coins—constitutes only a small percentage of the money supply, which is predominantly made up of accounts in banks. The predominant medium of exchange among both businesses and households is the check; cash is seldom used except in small transactions.

How is money created? Very simply, it is created by banks making loans. Assume that a bank makes a loan of $100,000 to a company that promises to repay after one year. The bank credits or increases the amount available in the company's checking account. Money supply increases by $100,000 as a result of this transaction.

What happens when the company repays the loan? Repayment is made by deducting $100,000 from the company's checking account. This action reduces the money supply. The principle is simple: making loans increases the money supply, repaying loans reduces it.

What restricts banks' capacity to make loans and create more money? Obviously, when individuals and companies have balances in their checking accounts, they write checks and withdraw cash from those accounts. So banks must maintain reserves either in the form of vault cash or deposits (checking accounts) with the Federal Reserve System. The Federal Reserve requires that banks maintain reserves equal to a specified percentage of their deposits. Deposits are backed by reserves; loans are not. The deposits represent a liability of the bank because the depositors can withdraw their money. It is the expansion or contraction of deposits that increases or decreases the money supply.

Excess reserves are a key determinant of the rate of growth of the money supply, for only when banks have excess reserves can they make loans. Whatever affects excess reserves also affects the money supply. However, new reserves are not created when checks written on one bank are deposited in another bank. In this case, one bank's expansion is counterbalanced by the other bank's creation of deposits. Checks written on banks within the system cancel each other out. It is only when excess reserves exist or are created by the Federal Reserve System that the money supply can increase.

Obviously, the Fed plays an extremely important role in the financial system. It controls money and has strong influence over whether credit is tight or easy, whether interest rates are high or low, and whether bond prices go up or down. This power is the reason so many "Fedwatchers" exist. The activities of the Fed are under constant scrutiny in the financial community and in media, and speculation about its motives abounds. Since it is money that drives the financial markets, bondholders should be aware of the role of the Fed.

7

MONEY SUPPLY

Money serves three vital functions in the economy:
1. *Medium of exchange.* Sellers accept money as a means of payment in market transactions. Money eliminates the need to barter when conducting business. In addition, individuals may specialize in a task in which they possess a comparative advantage since money can serve as payment in exchange for their labor.
2. *Standard of value.* Money provides for the measurement of the relative worth of diverse goods and services. Money is the common denominator by which goods and services can be compared. Two products can easily be compared based upon a single characteristic—the amount of money required to buy each.
3. *Store of value.* Money is a store of value, or purchasing power. It is the most liquid asset and is the most widely accepted form of wealth that can be exchanged for goods and services.

Defining Money Supply. The definition of the money supply causes economists continuing problems.

The Federal Reserve has periodically adjusted its definitions of money because of the emergence of new types of financial instruments such as negotiable orders of withdrawal (NOW) accounts, repurchase agreements (RPs or REPOs), and money market deposit accounts (MMDAs). Currently, the Fed has subdivided the money supply into four categories: M1, M2, M3, and L.

M1 is currency in circulation plus all checking accounts including those that pay interest, such as NOW accounts. M1 is the narrowest definition of the money supply, representing money primarily held to carry out transactions, including cash held in NOW accounts. NOW accounts are interest-bearing savings accounts on which checks may be written, and they are issued by thrift institutions. The greatest portion of this amount, over 70%, represents demand deposits, while less than 30% consists of currency and coin.

M2 expands M1 to include items that are not quite as liquid, including:

1. RPs, or REPOs, issued by commercial banks
2. Certain overnight Eurodollars (those issued by Caribbean branches of member banks) held by U.S. nonbank residents
3. Money market mutual fund (MMMF) balances
4. Money market deposit accounts (MMDAs)
5. Savings and small-denomination time deposits (less than $100,000) at all depository institutions

RPs, or REPOs, are agreements made by banks to sell government securities to customers and, simultaneously, to contract to repurchase the same securities at a price that includes accumulated interest. Since businesses cannot use NOW accounts, RPs offer a way to earn interest on idle cash. Eurodollars are short-term deposits at foreign banks or foreign branches of U.S. banks that are outside the U.S. Time deposits consist of savings certificates and small certificates of deposit (CDs). The owner of a CD is given a receipt indicating the amount deposited, the interest to be paid, and the maturity date. Money Market Deposit Accounts (MMDAs) are offered by banks and thrift institutions. They provide a market rate of interest, but usually require a minimum balance and a limit on the number of monthly transactions. Money market mutual funds are mutual funds that invest only in short-term credit instruments. Frequently they provide for check-writing privileges, with limits on the amount of the checks.

M3 and L. The broadest measure of the money supply is M3, which adds to M2 other liquid assets that are held predominantly by wealthy individuals or institutions. Examples include:

1. Time deposits and certain other instruments through which funds are loaned in large denominations ($100,000 or more) to depository institutions
2. Eurodollars held by U.S. residents
3. Shares in money market funds that are generally restricted to institutions

Debt by depository institutions in these forms represents funds that can be readily managed and varied in line with changes in fund needs.

The Fed also publishes a broader measure of liquidity called L. This measure includes a variety of short-term market instruments. Examples are:

1. Bankers acceptances
2. Commercial paper
3. Marketable Treasury and agency obligations with original maturities of less than 12 months

This measure has not served as a target for monetary policy because data on it are not available promptly.

Significance of the Money Supply. The supply of money is of crucial importance to economic activity. The money supply is one of the most useful leading indicators (indicators that foreshadow future economic activity). In addition, it is also used by many analysts for insight into the future course of bond prices. Changes in the total money supply and the rate at which it increases or decreases affect important economic variables such as inflation, interest rates, total employment, and gross national product. The control of the money supply is the primary responsibility of the Fed. The Fed manages the money supply through its control over bank reserves (see previous key). An increase in the money supply relative to demand for it causes interest rates to fall, stimulating investment spending, output, and employment. This relationship may be expressed as follows:

- ↑ Fed Reserves
- ↑ Bank lending
- ↑ Money supply
- ↓ Interest rates
- ↑ Economic activity

A decrease in money supply has the opposite effect:

- ↓ Fed Reserves
- ↓ Bank lending
- ↓ Money supply
- ↑ Interest rates
- ↓ Economic activity

Particularly when resources are fully employed, an increasing money supply has inflationary consequences. When more money exists than is needed to carry out transactions, prices rise. Money supply is closely tracked because it is a leading indicator of inflation. However, inflation doesn't immediately follow an acceleration in money supply growth; the process has historically taken one and one-half to two years. Nor does an increase in the money supply always foreshadow an increase in inflation; the 1983 bulge in money supply was not followed by a surge in inflation. It is possible that monetary indicators became less reliable in predicting future inflation with the introduction of new financial instruments such as NOW accounts, RPs, and MMDAs.

Reporting the M's. The money supply numbers are reported each Thursday afternoon. "Fed watchers" closely analyze this report for clues to the direction of monetary policy. Although M1 receives the greatest attention in the media, M2 is more closely watched by most economists. M2 is also the money supply number included in the leading economic indicators published by the U.S. Department of Commerce.

8

INFLATION

The greatest risk to the market value of most bonds is inflation. Since bonds have set interest rates and pay back the principal at a future date, an increase in inflation will depress the prices of existing bonds. Over the past 60 years, the real rate of return (the return adjusted for inflation) on bonds has been only about 2%. Meanwhile, the real rate of return on common stock has been about 7%. Even with the greater risk involved in holding common stock, the disparity in the return between the two investments clearly favors common stock. But investors do learn from experience, and current bond returns discount the higher rates of inflation endemic to our economy. With inflation running about 4-5% and returns on investment grade bonds around 9-10%, the real return of 5% provides adequate, if not generous, inflation protection.

Investors interested in anticipating the future rate of inflation should watch the trend in unit labor costs. Unit labor cost measures labor cost per unit of output, and the trend in this figure reflects how much added labor is required to produce an additional unit of output. This trend is probably the best harbinger of future inflation.

Measuring Inflation. If inflation is defined as a rise in the general level of prices, how is it measured? This problem is easily solved when referring to the price change of one product or service, but it becomes trickier when dealing with a large number of economic goods, some with prices that have risen faster than others. Realistically, price changes for all the goods produced by the economy cannot be computed. Instead, a representative market basket of goods is selected and the price changes in that basket over time are computed. This calculation is obtained by using a price index that compares the current cost of the market basket of goods to the cost of those goods in the base year. Hence, the price index is derived as follows:

$$\text{Price index} = \frac{\text{Current cost of market basket}}{\text{Cost of basket in base year}} \times 100$$

One way to gain an appreciation for the effect of inflation is to employ the "rule of 70." This method provides an approximate measure of the number of years required for the price level to double. The number 70 is divided by the annual rate of inflation:

$$\text{Number of years required for prices to double} = \frac{70}{\text{annual rate of inflation}}$$

For example, the price level will double in approximately 14 years if the inflation rate is 5% per year. Similarly, inflation of 10% per year means the price level will double in only 7 years.

Prominent Price Indexes. Three price indexes calculated by government statisticians receive a great deal of attention in the financial press: the consumer price index (CPI), the producer price index (PPI), and the gross national product (GNP) deflator. Each of these indexes measures the average price change for the goods and services that comprise the index. The changes in these indexes are highly correlated over time, and each reveals the persistence of inflation in recent economic history.

The Consumer Price Index. The CPI is the most widely cited index. It attempts to measure changes in the prices of goods and services purchased by urban consumers. The Bureau of Labor Statistics computes the index based upon data collected in 85 cities from nearly 25,000 sources. The index reflects price changes of approximately 400 goods and services comprising seven broad categories: food, clothing, housing, transportation, medical care, entertainment, and other. The CPI is considered to be the most reliable measure of changes in the cost of living for most American families. Prices for the CPI's base year 1967, have been set at 100. Each year since then the CPI has increased. For example, the CPI measured 311.1 in 1984, meaning the general level of prices as measured by the CPI more than tripled in the period from 1967 to 1984. CPI is calculated and reported each month.

Producer Price Index. The PPI, formerly called the Wholesale Price Index, measures changes in the average prices of goods received by producers of commodities, in all stages of processing, in primary or wholesale markets. It measures the change in prices paid by businesses. The "market basket" for calculating the PPI consists of about 2800 items purchased by producers and manufacturers, including crude, intermediate, and finished goods.

Because primary products included in the PPI are processed into finished goods distributed to retail markets, many analysts believe that changes in the PPI precede changes in the CPI. For this reason, the PPI is closely followed as an indicator of consumer prices. However, this relationship does not always hold true. Because the PPI does not include services, the price changes of the two indexes may not correlate. For instance, in a period of rapidly rising wages the price of services will increase at a faster rate than the price of goods because wages are a very large component in the cost of providing services.

Gross National Product Deflator. The GNP deflator is the most broadly based of the price level indicators. The CPI measures price changes for goods and services that households purchase for their own use. However, in the U.S. economy, household consumption is less than two thirds of total output, or gross national product (GNP). The remainder of the output is accounted for by government, investment by business, and the foreign sector. The GNP deflator is the most comprehensive index because it measures what happens to the prices of all final goods and services. As such, it is probably the best measure of overall price changes in the U.S. economy.

The GNP deflator is calculated as a byproduct of the calculation of current and real GNP. It is obtained by dividing current-year quantities at current-year prices by current-year quantities at base-year prices. The base year is currently 1982. Unlike the CPI and the PPI, which are reported monthly, the GNP deflator is calculated and reported quarterly.

Inflation and Investment Returns. Inflation impacts various investments differently. An asset that rises in price as fast or faster than the general level of prices is a good inflation hedge. Research indicates that, as a general proposition, lower inflation leads to higher returns for stocks and bonds, while higher inflation reduces returns on stocks and bonds. Bonds with longer-term maturities are particularly risky when inflation unexpectedly heats up. However, when inflation is subsiding, bonds with longer-term maturities are the best bet to lock in the high rates of interest.

9

BOND RATINGS

Any decision to purchase a corporate bond must be preceded by a knowledge of the bond's rating. A bond rating tells investors the probability of timely repayments of principal and interest. To minimize exposure to default as much as possible, bond investors watch bond ratings very closely. The two most prominent ratings agencies are Moody's Investors Service and Standard & Poor's Corporation. The ratings provide a measure of the relative ease with which a corporation can pay interest and repay principal. Before issuing a rating, the agencies must evaluate the financial health of the corporation by looking at evidence such as the firm's financial statements. The agencies continue to monitor the financial health of the organization even after the bonds have been issued. Frequently, they revise ratings in response to changes in the financial position of the issuer.

Symbols. Although the symbols may look different, they have virtually the same meaning. Moody's ratings for corporate bonds are, in descending order of quality: Aaa, Aa, A, Baa, Ba, B, Caa, Ca, and C.

Standard & Poor's ratings are: AAA, AA, A, BBB, BB, B, CCC, CC, C, and D.

The first four categories, AAA (Aaa) through BBB (Baa), represent investment grade securities. Institutional investors usually restrict their bond purchases to those top four categories. AAA (Aaa) bonds are judged to be of the best quality with an extremely strong capacity to pay interest and repay principal. The BBB (Baa) designation indicates only an adequate capacity to pay interest and repay principal. In addition to the above ratings, Moody's uses the symbols Aa1, A1, Baa1, Ba1, and B1 to identify the bonds in those groups that possess the strongest investment attributes, while Standard & Poor's uses plus or minus signs to provide a finer calibration within a category.

Bonds whose ratings are less than BBB (Baa)—BB, B, CCC, CC—are considered to be speculative, which means that the issuer's ability to meet interest payments and repay principal is not at all certain. These bonds are frequently referred to as "junk bonds" due to their high yield and risk. The word "junk" in this context can be a misnomer. Investments in these securities can provide excellent returns for those willing to assume the additional risk. However, bonds rated D are in default and payment of interest and/or repayment of principal is in arrears.

Caveat. Bond ratings provide a general guide to bond buyers. A rating is not a recommendation to purchase, sell, or hold a security. One should never rely only on these ratings when making a decision to buy or sell bonds. One potential problem is that bond ratings are slow to change even after significant corporate news has been reported. The quality of a bond can deteriorate overnight because of a sudden takeover, leveraged buyout, or corporate restructuring. Bond ratings should be used with other sources of information in making investment decisions.

10

BOND YIELDS

The interest rate or yield of a bond is expressed in several different ways, which can lead to some confusion among investors. To understand how the prices of bonds are determined, you must understand the three basic types of yield. When a newly issued bond is selling at par or face value ($1000), its coupon rate, current yield, and yield to maturity are all equal. But this concurrence of values is not common, except when bonds are close to maturity. Mostly, these securities trade above or below their face value.

Coupon (Nominal) Yield. The term coupon yield is used to describe a bond's percentage yield based on par value. If a bond has a par value of $1000 and pays interest at a rate of 9%, the coupon yield is 9%, meaning that interest income will be $90 a year on the bond. Since the coupon percentage rate and the principal do not change for the term of the bond, the coupon yield does not change either.

Current Yield. Once a bond has been issued, its price begins to fluctuate according to its demand and supply and changes in the general level of interest rates. If interest rates increase, the $1,000 bond with a coupon rate of 9% will decline in price. Suppose its price declined to $950. The investor is still entitled to the $90 yearly interest. The current yield is obtained by dividing a bond's coupon rate by its current price. In this case, $90 divided by $950 results in a 9.5% current yield. The current yield is thus higher than the coupon yield if a bond is purchased below par and lower if you buy the bond above par.

Yield to Maturity (YTM). The current yield only measures today's return. It does not reflect the total return, which includes the difference between the purchase price of the bond and the principal repayment at maturity. Someone who pays $950 for a $1000 bond will receive $1000 at maturity. The total return comprises both the interest and the $50 gain in price if held to maturity.

When referring to yield, bond traders generally mean yield to maturity. Because the YTM assesses the effect of principal, coupon rate, and time to maturity on a bond's actual yield, it enables investors and traders to compare bonds with different coupon rates and terms. Thus, it is a prime factor in setting the market value of bonds. It explains why investors buy short-term discount bonds with low coupon rates and long-term premium bonds with high coupons. Thus, investors must be attentive to the YTM. For traders, who do not intend to hold the bonds to maturity, the current yield is generally the most important yield figure.

Although the exact computation of YTM is complex, the YTM for a discount bond is easily approximated using the following steps:
1. Subtract the purchase price ($950) from par ($1000) to arrive at the discount of $50.
2. Divide the resulting figure ($50) by the number of years to maturity (10) to obtain an annualized

gain ($5).
3. Add the annual gain ($5) to the yearly interest ($90) to obtain a total return ($95).
4. Add the current price ($950) to the face amount ($1000) and divide by 2, resulting in $975.
5. Divide the result of step 3 ($95) by the result of step 4 ($975), obtaining a 9.95% YTM.

11

CONVERTIBLE BONDS

A convertible bond is a bond that can be exchanged into shares of common stock under specified terms. Once the bond has been exchanged or converted into common stock, it cannot be converted back. Like a straight bond, a convertible bond provides the investor with a fixed interest payment. What makes these securities interesting investments is that the conversion feature gives holders of these securities a chance to reap the benefits of rising stock prices.

Like other bonds, convertibles generally have a face or par value of $1000 for each bond. This means that the corporation promises to pay back $1000 to the holder when the bond matures. In addition, the corporation also pays a fixed rate of interest, which typically is less than the interest on a nonconvertible bond because of the value of the conversion feature. Investors are willing to accept a lower rate of interest in return for the opportunity to participate in the appreciation of the common stock.

Advantages to the Issuer. Although the advantages of convertible securities to investors are well documented, what reasons do companies have for issuing them? First, as previously indicated, the interest that companies have to pay is lower than the interest on nonconvertible or straight bond issues. The interest savings is usually at least 100 basis points (1%), and in many cases it is significantly greater than that. This difference exists even though straight bonds have prior claim to interest and assets upon dissolution. This subordination feature means that the bond rating of convertibles is typically one class lower than nonconvertible bonds of the same company.

Second, convertible securities are often issued by corporations experiencing financial problems and having difficulty selling preferred stock or bonds. The conversion feature makes these issues more attractive to investors, especially those willing to assume risks.

Third, the issuance of convertible securities does not seem to upset existing stockholders as much as the addition of additional shares of common stock. Corporations have found this to be true even though the conversion of these securities will dilute the voting control and share in the corporation's earnings of the common stockholders. But that potential lies in the future, and most U.S. shareholders focus on the present.

Advantages to the Investor. These securities combine the advantages of the safety and fixed income of bonds or preferred stock with the potential for capital appreciation from holding the common stock. The owners of these securities can participate in the rising price of the common stock by converting the security into that common stock. Actually, holders of these securities do not have to convert their securities to participate in rising stock prices. Typically, the price of the convertible security will rise with the price of the stock, although it never rises as much. On the other hand, if the stock price declines, the price of the convertible will also decline, again by not as much. In this case, the interest specified on the convertible bond or the dividend on the convertible preferred stock serves to brake the decline in price. Therefore, holders of convertible securities have good reasons to stay with the security and not convert.

Meanwhile, even if the stock price languishes, holders of those securities receive their guaranteed fixed return. Many of the companies issuing these securities are smaller companies whose common stock is speculative in nature. Typically, many of these companies have a low dividend yield on their common stock, which makes the common stock an unattractive investment for those investors for whom current return is important. Convertible securities provide these investors with an alternative way to participate in the possible appreciation of the stock while earning a good current return.

Computation. An examination of a convertible issue traded on the NYSE will serve to illustrate these concepts. This security is reported in a table called New York Exchange Bonds, where convertible securities are denoted by the initials "cv" in the current yield column.

Compaq Computer has a convertible bond which sold for $143 on June 29, 1989. The conversion rate is the number of common shares received by converting one bond. Compaq Computer CV bonds are each convertible into 1,538 shares. The conversion value is the price of the common stock multiplied by the conversion rate. In this instance, the conversion value is 1,538 times the market price of the common stock on June 29, 1989 of $90 for a conversion value of 138.4. The premium is the measure of the percentage by which the CV bond is selling above its actual conversion value. The premium is determined by taking the price of the bond ($143), subtracting the conversion value ($138.4), and dividing the remainder ($4.6) by the conversion value ($138.4). In this case, the premium is 3.3%.

Caveat. Many convertible bonds are issued by financially weak corporations that might not be able to raise funds otherwise. Remember that if such a firm goes bankrupt, the convertible bondholders' claims on any assets of the corporation are subordinate to the claims of the straight bondholders. Thus, convertible bondholders may not receive anything. In other cases, the convertible bonds of strong corporations may be in demand at their initial sale and often carry excessive premiums in the open market. Investors should realize that the hybrid nature of these securities makes them difficult to evaluate. Diversification and assessment of credit quality are essential. For these reasons, most investors are better off purchasing mutual funds rather than trying to buy convertibles on their own. Some of the leading convertible bond funds include:

Fidelity Convertible	(800) 544-6666
Dreyfus Convertible Securities	(800) 645-6561
Vanguard Convertible	(800) 662-7447
American Capital Harbor	(800) 421-5666

As a general rule, convertible securities are callable, which means a company can call in the security and redeem it for cash. But such bonds are seldom ever actually redeemed. The purpose of the call provision is to force conversion of the issue when the conversion value of the security is significantly above the call price. If the convertible security is called when the market value of the stock is greater than the conversion value of the bond, conversion is advisable.

12

ZERO COUPON BONDS

Zero coupon bonds (zeros) are bonds that pay no interest but are sold at deep discounts from face value ($1000). These bonds are particularly appealing to investors who think interest rates are at or near their peak. They are called zeros because they are stripped of their interest coupons (interest is not paid) which is added to the principal every six months. The advantage to the investor is that current interest rates can be locked in until the bonds mature. These bonds accrue interest as if it were paid every six months and reinvested at the yield quoted when purchased. Generally, other bonds provide interest every six months, but if interest rates are declining, the interest could not be reinvested at yields as high as when the bonds were purchased.

When zeros mature, the investor receives the interest in a lump sum payment. The difference between the price paid initially and the amount received at maturity is the return on the investment (yield to maturity). For example, a zero coupon corporate with a maturity value of $10,000, that yields 9% and matures in ten years, recently cost $4146.

Taxation of Zero Coupon Bond Interest. Although interest is not distributed to holders of zeros, it is subject to taxation. Investors must pay income taxes annually as though they had actually received the interest. Zeros are a useful investment for IRAs, Keoghs, and other tax-advantaged retirement plans because the investor can avoid paying taxes on interest not received.

Caveat. Because of the lack of cash interest payments to dampen market swings, zeros tend to be more volatile in price than other bonds. If interest rates rise, prices of zeros can fall dramatically. Investors purchasing zeros should intend to hold them to maturity.

Investors often underestimate the risk of trading zeros before maturity. Zeros, like other bonds, command higher prices when market rates fall. The difference is that zeros are much more volatile. Even a nominal market increase can be disastrous. The numbers below give you some indication of the extreme risks of trading zeros.

When Bonds Mature

	5 years	10 years	20 years
To get $1,000 at maturity on a zero coupon bond yielding 8%, an investor pays:	$675.56	$456.39	$208.29
If rates fall to 7%, the value rises to:	$708.92	$502.57	$252.57
	(+5%)	(+10%)	(+21%)
If rates rise to 9%, the value falls to:	$643.93	$414.64	$171.93
	(−5%)	(−9%)	(−17%)

Note that the longer the maturity, the greater the risk of loss as well as gain. Since few, if any, investors can accurately anticipate interest rates, you have to be prepared for extreme fluctuations in the price of zero-coupon bonds.

Aggressive investors who want to gamble on interest rate swings use the Benham zero coupon funds of Benham Capital Management Group as a vehicle. These funds allow investors to switch in and out without incurring extra costs. Most investors should not invest in zeros outside of IRAs or other tax-deferred vehicles. For those who are interested, the following criteria should be observed:

1. Purchase zeros with different maturities to diversify interest rate risk.
2. If your guess on interest rates proves wrong, be prepared to hold on.
3. Don't buy zeros of financially weak corporations. If the issuer defaults after you purchased the bond, your losses exceed a straight bond since you've received no interest meanwhile.

Zeros are denoted by the initials "zr" in the New York Exchange Bonds Table.

13

TIMING BOND
PURCHASES

Four simple yardsticks are available to assist individual investors in deciding whether or not to purchase long-term corporate bonds. Individuals should not rely on just one rule but use them as a group to validate their conclusions. If the rules don't provide consistent answers, caution is advised.

The Yield Curve. The yield curve is a graphic representation of the relationship between short-term and long-term interest rates (discussed in the next key). As a simple rule of thumb, bonds will generally perform well if long-term rates offer a significant premium over short-term rates. A narrow spread indicates insufficient reward for the extra maturity risk. Experts suggest subtracting the yield on three-month Treasury bills from the yield on long-term Treasury bonds. If the difference is more than three percentage points, bonds are a good investment. A difference of less than 1.5 percentage points favors short-term securities.

Real Yields. Real yields are bond yields minus the rate of inflation. The usual approach is to take the yield on the Treasury's 30-year bond and subtract the latest 12-month rate of increase in producer prices. A difference of 5% or more is a good spread, indicating bonds are good buys. A margin of 2% or less is a negative sign. When real bond yields have been less than 2%, investors have suffered principal losses seven out of eight years.

Real Yield Trends. The trend in real (inflation-adjusted) yields is also important. If real yields have declined over the preceding 12 months, bonds are a poor investment. If they have risen, that's a positive sign. Specifically, experts suggest that a real yield increase of four percentage points or more over the preceding 12 months represents a buy signal, while a four-percentage-point decrease over that time period is a sell signal.

Inflation Trend. What is the trend of inflation? An increase in the rate of inflation portends trouble for the bond market, while a declining rate of inflation bolsters interest in bonds. One suggested procedure is to compare the latest 12-month rise in the producer price index with the 12-month rise in the index six months previously. If the latest number is higher, caution is indicated.

14

YIELD CURVE

A yield curve is a graph that illustrates the relationship between rates of return and maturities of similar fixed-income bonds. Different yield curves can be derived for Treasury issues, issues of government agencies, prime grade municipals, AAA corporates, etc. For a given bond issuer, the relationship between the interest rates of bonds and their years to maturity (assuming that the bonds differ in only these two respects) is called the term structure of interest rates, or the yield curve.

Simply put, the yield curve reflects the difference between short-term and long-term interest rates. Drawing the term structure is relatively simple. The different yields (not coupon rates) are represented on the vertical axis, the years to maturity are shown on the horizontal axis. The term structure of interest rates is a static function that relates the term to maturity to the yield to maturity at a given point in time. The quality of the issues must be held constant —this is why the yield curves are usually constructed using Treasury securities, which represent the highest-quality investment.

Types of Yield Curves. Yield curves can assume different shapes. The behavior of yield curves over time is quite fluid. Four different types of yield curves are shown below.

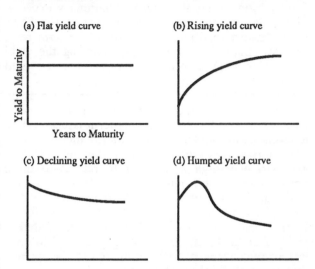

(a) Flat yield curve

(b) Rising yield curve

(c) Declining yield curve

(d) Humped yield curve

The yield curve demonstrates graphically what market participants are willing to pay for short-term, intermediate-term, and long-term debt instruments. Generally, rates rise with the length of the investment. The yield curve usually slopes upward, as in (b). The logic is simple: If investors commit their money for longer periods, they take more risk and demand greater returns. For a relatively brief period in late 1988 and early 1989, U.S. interest rates had an inverted yield curve: Long-term rates were lower than short-term rates. Such inversions occur only rarely—nine in the last 35 years.

It is generally agreed that the 1988-1989 yield curve

inversion was caused by the Federal Reserve's vigorous stand against inflation. The Fed restricted the growth of the money supply and raised the key federal funds rate, the interest rate that banks charge each other for lending excess reserves (see Key 6). The Fed's action raised short-term inflationary expectations but gave the market confidence in the Fed's battle against inflation. As a result, long-term rates rose less than short-term rates, inverting the yield curve. Curve (c) is an example of an inverted yield curve.

A humped yield curve (d) occurs when yields on intermediate-term issues rise above those on short-term issues and the rates on long-term issues decline to levels below those for the short-term, then level out. The humped yield curve is formed when interest rates are extremely high and about to retreat to more normal levels. A flat yield curve (a), where short-term rates equal long-term rates, is a rare occurrence. The slope of the line tends to level off after 15 years for all of the yield curves. After this point, the different yields that exist with longer maturities tend to have less significance, especially compared to the spreads that occur at the short-term end.

Trading Implications. The yield curve has definite trading implications for bondholders. A descending yield curve usually indicates that the economy will weaken and that lower yields are more likely to occur than higher yields. If investors anticipate this scenario, then they should purchase long-term bonds to lock in the higher yields and, perhaps, to profit from the higher bond prices that are likely in the future.

When the yield curve is upward sloping, some bond portfolio managers attempt to increase their yields by adopting a strategy called "riding the yield curve." This strategy involves the purchase of intermediate or long-term bonds. These investments are maintained to obtain the capital gains that occur as the bonds move closer to their maturity dates and thus "ride down the yield curve" to the lower interest rates that are available when they become short-term bonds. In other words, the bond investor earns capital gains resulting from the lower yields obtainable as the bonds move along their yield curve toward the maturity date. To implement this strategy, the shape of the yield curve must be continuously monitored because the level of interest rates may rise or the short-end of the yield curve may swing upward.

15

CALL FEATURE

Most corporate bonds are sold with a "call" feature that allows the firm to redeem the bonds before maturity. Bond issuers use this feature to protect themselves from paying interest rates greater than current prevailing interest rates. Companies call in bonds when general interest rates are lower than the coupon rate on the bond, similar to a homeowner's refinancing a house when home mortgage rates drop.

When a bond issuer does exercise its right to redeem a bond prior to maturity, it is often required by the terms of the bond to pay a penalty to the bondholders in the form of a premium in excess of the bond's par value. The size of this premium will vary according to the length of time the call occurs after the issuance of a bond.

For example, assume an 11% $1000 bond is yielding 2% more than the current interest rate on equivalent bonds. If the call price is set at "110" (i.e., $1100), the issuer pays $1100 for each bond and issues new bonds yielding 9% interest. The proceeds of the new issue are used to redeem the old issue, and the issuer now pays less interest for the borrowed funds.

Action on Callable Bonds. In the period from 1990 to 1994 many billions of dollars of corporate bonds will be eligible to be called away from investors, more than ever before in market history. The reason for the wave of calls is the surge in bond issuance in the early 1980s, when interest rates climbed to double digits. Firms chose to pay the increased rates on long-term bonds rather than the still-higher rates on short-term securities, which during one period exceeded 20%. Corporate bond issuance climbed to about $92 billion a year from half that pace in the late 1970s.

This combination of more bonds being sold at a time of peaking rates initially proved stunningly profitable for investors, who were earning double-digit yields on presumably long-term investments. Investors who bought higher-yielding bonds years after they were issued frequently paid a price exceeding the face or par value of the bond ($1000). For example, a $1000 bond sold originally with a double-digit coupon rate might be sold today for $1150. That would give the investor who bought the bond after it was originally issued a return similar to the returns now being offered on new bonds. However, the bond is worth the premium price only if the investor is assured of receiving the interest payments for a number of years. The danger for the investor is the risk of incurring a capital loss if the bond is called. The call price is based on par value plus a premium. The premium can be a set amount or based on a declining scale, with greater premiums required for calling in during earlier years. For example, Ford Motor Company's call price for its 9.15% 2004 bonds in 1990 is 102.50% of principal amount and will gradually decline each year. In 1998, the call price will be 100.25% of the principal amount.

Investors should expect bonds to be called when current interest rates are several percentage points below the coupon rate. A call on a bond is almost always a negative development for a bondholder. Generally, bonds are called when rates are declining and investors would prefer to lock in the higher yield by keeping the bond. The disadvantage for investors is that they will have to reinvest the funds received at lower interest rates.

Investors need to be aware of the call features of the bonds they acquire. Call features are not specified in the financial sections of newspapers. However, this information does appear in Standard & Poor's *Bond Guide,* on the back of bond certificates, and in final bond prospectuses.

To protect yourself from calls, you should purchase either newly issued or recently issued bonds, which often cannot be called for five or ten years. Another strategy is to buy "discount" bonds, which sell for less than par because they pay below-market interest rates. These bonds offer a better investment than premium bonds for investors who want to lock in a return for as long as possible because their low stated rates make them less likely to be called.

16

READING BOND QUOTES

Many bonds have thin markets with only a limited amount of trading. Quotes for these issues are unlikely to be listed. Prices of many corporate bonds are listed in a table called New York Exchange Bonds, which covers bonds bought and sold on the New York Stock Exchange (NYSE). The NYSE bond market offers investors a broad selection of some 4000 bonds with an aggregate par value of more than $300 billion. However, only a small proportion of bond trading takes place on the New York Stock Exchange. Most bond trading is over the counter among securities dealers.

A typical listing will look as follows:

Bonds	Cur Yld	Vol	Close	Net Chg
IBM9s98	9.3	90	97¼	+ ¼

The first column shows the name of the issuer, the original interest rate (coupon rate), and the year of maturity (when the bond becomes due). The "s" is there for ease of pronunciation in rates without a fraction. Thus, 9s98 means "nines of ninety-eight," or 9% bonds due in 1998. (An IBM bond maturing in 1992 that pays 9.625% is designated IBM9⅝.) The second column gives the current yield, or the interest obtained by dividing the original interest rate by the latest price. In this case, each bond pays $90 annual interest, so the current yield is 9.3%. The third column indicates the volume of trading, in thousands of dollars. In this case, $90,000 was traded. The last two columns provide the closing price and the change from the previous day, which is an increase of $25 per bond. Sometimes the table will also show the daily high and low price and, at the left, the 12-month high and low.

Bond prices are quoted as a percentage of face value. In our example, the closing price of 97¼ means that the actual price of the bond is 97.25% times $1000 face value = $975 for each bond. In a discussion of bonds, the term "basis point" is often used. A basis point is ¹⁄₁₀₀th of one percent and is a convenient way to discuss changes in yields. For example, an increase in yield from 9.5% to 10% is an increase of 50 basis points.

At the top of the New York Exchange Bonds Table in *The Wall Street Journal* is data on the year's volume to date and a market diary. A set of Dow Jones Averages for bond prices is also included. The main index includes 20 bonds. Component indexes are included for the 10 industrials and the 10 utilities. The New York table is followed by a short listing of bonds traded on the American Stock Exchange.

A further listing of the prices of 20 representative, actively traded corporate bonds, compiled by First Boston Corp., appears daily in the Bond Market Data Bank. The Data Bank also lists the performance of several other indexes made up of various categories of corporate and convertible bond issues. The Merrill Lynch Corporate Master Index, for example, represents a portfolio of about 4400 nonconvertible bonds with remaining maturities of at least one year, a minimum of $1 million outstanding, and an average credit rating of A-1.

17

MUTUAL FUNDS

For those investors who lack the time or expertise to manage an investment portfolio, an excellent investment alternative is to purchase shares in mutual funds. A mutual fund is a pool of commingled funds contributed by many investors and managed by a professional fund manager in exchange for a fee. Many mutual funds that invest in corporate bonds are available to meet the needs of investors.

Advantages of Mutual Funds. Mutual funds offer four major advantages that make them attractive for investors:

1. *Diversification.* A diversified portfolio is very difficult to achieve when funds are limited. A mutual fund offers the investor the opportunity to participate in an investment pool that can contain hundreds of different securities.

2. *Professional Management.* Many investors lack the time or expertise to supervise their investments. Mutual funds are managed by professionals who have the training and experience to make judgments about bond selection and timing.

3. *Liquidity.* Funds can be easily traded. Quotes on the current value of funds are readily available in the financial section of most newspapers.
4. *Constant Supervision.* Mutual fund managers handle all the details of managing the portfolio including arranging for dividend payments and updating the performance and tax record for each investor. In addition, funds permit the automatic reinvestment of interest for compounding.

Disadvantages of Mutual Funds. Not all the earnings of mutual funds flow into the accounts of the investors. Management fees and other expenses take around 1% of a fund's income. In addition, buying into a "load" fund can result in an immediate decrease in an investor's capital, as explained below.

Load and No-Load Funds. Mutual funds can be divided into load and no-load funds. This distinction is based upon whether or not they charge a sales fee when the fund is initially issued. The fee, or commission, is known as a "load." A load fund charges up to 8.5% of net asset value that is deducted from the amount of the investment. Thus, a $10,000 purchase of an 8% load fund means that $800 is deducted as a fee and only $9,200 is actually invested. Load funds are available only through stockbrokers, financial advisors, or other sales representatives.

No-load funds are typically purchased directly from the fund. No initial sales charge is deducted from the investment, so $10,000 invested in a no-load fund means the entire $10,000 is actually invested. The performance of load funds has been compared with the performance of no-load funds, and there is no evidence that on average, load funds perform better than no-load funds. An investor interested in short-term profits should unquestionably avoid high-load funds.

Objectives of Different Funds. Investors should remember that the prices of bond funds will fluctuate in response to changes in interest rates. Investors also need to consider maturities when purchasing bond funds. In general, the longer the maturity of the bonds in a fund's portfolio, the more volatile the fund's price. Long-term bond funds are riskier than those funds that concentrate on shorter-term securities. Investors who want to maximize gains if rates drop should purchase long-term bond funds.

The maturity structure (average maturities) of many funds is frequently described by the name of the fund. Generally, a short-term portfolio has a weighted average maturity of less than three years. Intermediate denotes an average maturity of three to ten years, and long-term is over ten years.

The most volatile funds are devoted to zero-coupon bonds, which pay no interest and are sold at a steep discount to face value (see Key 12). Zero-coupon bond funds are frequently near the very top or the very bottom of quarterly bond-fund performance ratings.

Bond funds can also be classified into high-grade bond funds and high-yield bond funds. High-grade bonds are those securities rated A or above. Typically, their yield will be 1% to 2% above Treasury bonds (the safest of all bonds). Despite this difference in yield, on a historical basis the overall risk of owning a diversified portfolio of high-grade bonds has not differed significantly from the risk involved in owning a portfolio of U.S. government securities.

On the other hand, high-yield bond funds invest in lower-rated corporate bonds that have a higher default risk and must offer higher yields to compensate for the greater risk. The yield of these funds historically has ranged from 3% to 6% above that of Treasury bonds, although the difference has recently exceeded 7%. These funds have declined in popularity with the increase in the risk of this segment of the bond market (discussed further in Key 20). They represent the only way that most investors should invest in high-risk bonds. Without the diversification offered by a fund that spreads its money among a great many different bonds, an investor in junk bonds would run the risk of losing everything.

Selecting Funds. The following criteria are recommended in purchasing bond funds:

1. Select only no-load funds that have been in existence for at least five years. This period is lengthy enough to include both good and bad years for bonds.
2. Buy only no-load funds with an expense ratio under 1%. It is difficult for performance to overcome high expense ratios. Fee tables are required by the SEC in all mutual fund prospectuses.
3. If you invest in high-yield or junk bond funds, it is important that the fund be well diversified. An appropriate number of issues would be at least 75 to 100.

18

UNIT INVESTMENT TRUSTS

Unit investment trusts (UITs) are fixed, closed-end portfolios in which investors can purchase units of participation for as little as $1000. They are fixed in the sense that the entire portfolio is accumulated at its beginning before sales to the public begin. Closed-end means there are a limited number of units for sale.

A UIT's portfolio remains the same except in a few exceptional circumstances, such as when a bond is called. Each type of trust is composed of one category of securities such as municipal bonds, certificates of deposit, utility common stocks, or corporate bonds. A unit represents functional ownership of all securities in the fund and entitles the owner to a proportionate share of the income produced by those securities. Interest or dividend income is usually distributed on a monthly basis. The principal is returned when the securities mature or are redeemed or sold, unless the investor sells the units before that time.

Advantages. UITs are not managed so there is little

or no management fee. Since the portfolio is fixed, you know exactly what you own. With few exceptions, the portfolio remains unchanged. Interest income is typically distributed on a monthly basis. All UITs have fixed lives, varying from a few months up to 30 years. At maturity, the bonds are sold and investors receive the proceeds.

Caveat. Investors should typically plan to purchase UITs as a long-term investment. The sales charges of from 2% to 5% reduce their value as a short-term investment. Investors should understand the fee structure and sales charges. The charges are usually up-front with no fees or penalties if sold before maturity. Determine if the broker or other selling agent maintains a secondary market so that the units can be redeemed before maturity.

Sponsors of UITs are brokerage firms. Traditionally, the two largest sponsors have been Merrill Lynch and John Nuveen & Company, although other brokerage firms have entered this market. Investors should not purchase a UIT only on the basis of advertised current return (the annual interest earnings divided by the offering price). Trusts can boost this current return by purchasing premium bonds, which pay higher interest but which cost more than face value. When these bonds are paid off, whether at maturity or when they are called (see Key 15), the proceeds will be less than what the trust paid for them. Thus, the long-term overall return of the fund will likely be lower than its advertised current yield. Investors should examine the list of bonds each trust holds in order to find out the quality of both the interest payments and the yield to maturity.

19

LEVERAGED BUYOUTS

Leveraged buyouts (LBOs) have been a dominant factor on the corporate financial landscape since 1984. In the 1980s, the dollar value of LBOs exceeded $200 billion. They included over 2800 companies—more than the 1700 companies listed on the New York Stock Exchange. The 1988 purchase of RJR Nabisco by the New York LBO firm of Kohlberg Kravis Roberts & Co. (KKR) for $24.7 billion intensified interest in LBOs and provoked concern about their merit. Corporations that previously had considered themselves too large for a takeover attempt now were implementing takeover defenses.

What Is a Leveraged Buyout (LBO)? A leveraged buyout is essentially a means of converting a publicly held company into a privately held company by buying out its shareholders with money borrowed using the company's assets as collateral. The money borrowed will ultimately be repaid from the cash flow of the business.

LBOs are often an alternative when management believes the price of the stock does not reflect the real value of the company. A typical LBO operates as follows: First, management decides the company would be better off privately held and makes an arrangement with an independent investment group (with financing connections) to form a new holding company. This holding company then buys out the original company's shareholders. After the buyout, the holding company and the original company merge to form a new company.

The new company's shares are sold to the original company's management, the independent investor group, and, often, the original company's shareholders. The new company borrows the remainder of the funds it needs for the buyout from a lending institution. Typically, 90% or more of the funds for LBOs are borrowed. The assets of the original company usually secure the debt, which is serviced from the old company's cash flow. The term "leveraged" is appropriate because the majority of the new company's capitalization is debt.

As an added inducement, the independent investor and the original company's shareholders often get warrants or options that enable them to increase their ownership in the new company. If the LBO is successful, the new owners eventually issue new shares in a public offering.

The key to profitability for the new owners is to whittle down the huge debt as quickly as possible. This goal is reached by selling assets and reducing overhead and inventories. If successful, the financial rewards can be awesome. The investors who put $80 million into Dr. Pepper in 1986 received more than $600 million in cash in 1988. A group led by William Simon after acquiring Gibson Greeting in a LBO subsequently took it public and made a 200-fold return. On the other hand, in the 1990s many LBOs began to fail, with enormous losses for bondholders and other investors in the new corporations.

Who Benefits and Who Loses? LBOs can rack up

stunning profits for the parties involved. The original shareholders receive a premium price for their stock and the opportunity to reinvest a portion of those profits in a successor company. For example, in 1989 RJR Nabisco shareholders received $90 for shares previously traded at $56. Management acquires ownership of the company it was previously running with a profit potential far exceeding their salaries. The lending institution obtains a high-yielding investment secured by the company's assets. In addition, a recent trend is for lending institutions to take an ownership stake in the deals they finance.

Even in the go-go 1980s, there were some big losers in the boom in LBOs. Besides the employees who lost their jobs as a result of restructuring and consolidations, the holders of investment-grade corporate bonds also often came out on the short end of these deals. LBOs involve massive debt that can cause the value of existing bonds to plunge. RJR Nabisco's huge leveraged buyout proposal caused RJR bonds to plummet as much as 15% in one week in October of 1988. The projected massive new debt transformed its bonds into high-yield, high-risk junk bonds. By early 1990 some junior RJR bonds were yielding over 20%. The fear of the impact of LBOs has affected the entire corporate bond market, raising yields on industrial bonds relative to other corporate issues.

The funds borrowed for LBOs are typically ten times the funds contributed as equity. Obviously, LBOs could not be undertaken without the assistance of financial institutions. The debt incurred typically consists of bank loans and junk bonds. The kicker in these deals is that the debt has to be repaid. The assumption is that interest and principal can be met with future cash flow. This optimism typically reflects a view of the future that others might not share: No recession will reduce cash flow, and no surge in interest rates will boost debt-service costs. The occurrence of either of these conditions would be disquieting for many LBOs. If both of these conditions occur, LBOs may default on their debt, leading to a chilling impact on the economy.

Recent Trends. The leveraged buyout business is facing more difficult times in the 1990s. The disarray in the junk bond market has noticeably slowed activity in the takeover arena. Junk bonds were a vital source of financing for many LBOs in the 1980s. The financial woes of Campeau Corp. and the bankruptcies or restructurings of Hillsborough Holdings, SCI Television, Leaseway, and other companies have cast a pall over this market. Further chilling investor interest is the bankruptcy of Drexel Burnham Lambert, the firm that established the modern junk bond market. Junk bond investors have disappeared, and junk bond prices have suffered steep declines.

But these difficulties will not stop LBO activity. Expect LBOs to be smaller and more conservatively financed in the 1990s. Leveraged firms must look beyond high-risk, high-yield bonds. Financing provided by the private placement market, which is dominated by insurance companies, will become more important, and the deals of the 1990s will feature more equity and less junk.

Despite excesses in the late 1980s, LBO activity has had a positive influence on American business. Management has been forced to focus upon enhancing shareholder value by streamlining operations and selling noncore businesses. A study of 76 large management buyouts from 1980 to 1986 by University of Chicago finance professor Steven Kaplan showed improvements in cash flow, operating income, and operating margins. With LBO equity investment funds totaling as high as $40 billion, LBOs will be a factor in the marketplace over the next decade.

20

JUNK BONDS

Many investors interested in high yields have purchased so-called junk bonds that yield substantially more returns than higher quality bonds. The differential yield advantage has historically been three to six percentage points above U.S. Treasury bonds, but this gap has widened recently to over 7%. However, this rarefied yield is the result of the recent steep price declines in the junk bond market.

In the period from 1980 to 1988, long-term junk bonds returned a compound average (capital gains and losses and interest combined) of 14%. This rate is 1.5% per year in excess of investment-grade corporates and nearly 3% better than Treasury bonds with comparable maturities. However, the returns since 1988 have plummeted. In 1989 widespread selling pushed junk bond prices down 4%, causing the average yield to move up to 15% in early 1990. By comparison, the Shearson Government/Corporate Bond Index climbed a healthy 14.2% in 1989.

Junk bonds are those bonds rated less than BBB by Standard & Poor's and less than Baa by Moody's. Ratings under Baa and BBB are considered to be speculative and not investment grade. Investment grade denotes obligations that are eligible for investment by various institutions such as banks, insurance companies, and savings and loans.

The Role of Michael Milken. It is fair to say that the now-bankrupt investment firm of Drexel Burnham Lambert and its highest paid officer, Michael Milken, created the junk-bond market. In the late 1960s, Milken began to study the market for depressed bonds of previously highly rated companies that were in financial difficulty. Despite the high yields, most investors avoided these bonds. But Milken's research showed that companies rarely defaulted on their bonds. During the early 1970s Milken produced a 50% annual profit trading junk bonds. By 1977 he decided to create a market for "original" junk—high-yielding bonds of young, promising companies in need of capital. Such a market offered unlimited opportunities for Drexel Burnham Lambert Inc., his employer, because relatively few companies would sell bonds not deemed investment grade by the ratings agencies. He persuaded smaller, younger companies that the sale of bonds yielding 13% when high-quality bonds were yielding 9% would benefit them financially. In turn, he convinced many investors that these 13% bonds were less risky than the yield might imply.

A turning point for Milken came in 1983, when he began to use junk bonds for hostile takeovers. The new breed of raiders, through the use of junk bonds, now had enough capital to go after the nation's largest companies. In 1982, the total volume of junk bond issuance was $2.5 billion. Four years later, junk bond issuances totaled a startling $34 billion. This activity coincided with the value of corporate mergers, which soared from $54 billion in 1982 to $173 billion in 1986.

And then the bubble burst. The stock market crashed in 1987, and the federal government indicted

Milken in 1988 on 90 counts of securities fraud. He soon lost his job at Drexel, which began a slide that culminated in its bankruptcy and liquidation in 1990.

Current Market for Junk Bonds. It is the worst of times for junk bond investors. The failures of Campeau Corp. and other companies, the bankruptcy of Drexel Burnham Lambert and the downgrading of RJR Nabisco's bonds by Moody's Investors Service have had a broad and indiscriminately negative effect on the junk bond market. More than $2.2 billion poured out of junk bond funds following the disclosures of the cash crunch at Campeau Corp.'s retailing units in the fall of 1989. The outflow continued in 1990. According to Donaldson, Lufkin & Jenrette, assets of Fidelity High Income Fund, T. Rowe Price High Yield Fund, and Vanguard Fixed Income: High Yield Bond Portfolio, the three largest no-load fixed income funds, fell 6% in January 1990 alone. These funds' assets were down by more than one-third from their peak in mid-1989 to early 1990. No one knows when or how this turmoil will end.

The junk bond market is not going to disappear. Junk bonds are a mature $200 billion dollar market that serves the important function of providing firms with sorely needed capital. Although junk bond issuances have plunged in 1990, eventually this market will stabilize. However, the 15% yield for B-rated bonds indicates very high risk for investors. There are concerns about junk bonds' liquidity, which has diminished sharply during the bear market in high yield bonds and since the departure of Drexel Burnham Lambert from this market. Investors should be wary of this market and invest in junk bonds only through a mutual fund, where risk is diversified by having a large number of junk bonds in the portfolio.

Junk Bond Returns. The yields on junk bond returns can run the gamut from 12% to 20%, although higher-quality junk bonds yield in the neighborhood of 12% to 15%. Yields on newly issued junk bonds are currently about seven percentage points higher than on seven-year Treasury notes. Individual investors should focus on larger, better capitalized issues and avoid the small, obscure issues that may be difficult to resell in the secondary market. Most investors should confine their junk bond investments to mutual funds that specialize in junk bonds.

Many investors don't understand a key difference between junk bonds and investment grade bonds. Unlike investment grade bonds, lower interest rates do not necessarily mean higher bond prices. Interest rates are less important than the performance of the economy in determining junk bond prices. Junk bonds are often issued by companies whose financial condition is weak. Many are issued to finance corporate takeovers and management-led buy-outs of stockholders. Their financial position is dominated by heavy debt. It is these firms' ability to generate cash flows that will determine whether or not their obligations can be satisfied.

When the economy is robust, junk bond prices tend to outperform other bonds. When the economy slows, however, junk bonds can plummet. Investors should understand that an economic downturn will depress corporate earnings, making it difficult for highly leveraged companies to meet their debt obligations. Junk bonds are more akin to common stock than investment grade bonds in that they respond more to changes in corporate earnings and cash flows than to interest rate changes.

21

JUNK BOND RISK

A great deal of debate has erupted recently over the investment merit of junk bonds. In early 1989 junk bonds yielded only 3.5 percentage points more than U.S. Treasury bonds. Within a year, the difference (spread) between junk bonds and Treasuries had doubled. The market has clearly become more gloomy about junk bond prospects. Is this pessimism over-done?

A study by Harvard professor Paul Asquith and two colleagues in 1989 concluded that the risk of junk bond defaults is significantly greater than previously acknowledged. They found that investors who bought and held a portfolio of all the junk bonds issued in 1977 and 1978 would have experienced a default rate of 34% by November 1, 1988. However, their study did not draw any conclusions about whether junk bonds were good investments.

In 1989 Moody's Investors Service released its own study analyzing junk bond defaults. Moody's found that an average of 3.3% of junk bonds defaulted each year between 1970 and 1988. This result compares with an annual default rate of .06% for investment grade (minimum BBB or Baa bond rating) bonds. Moody's noted that annual default rates of junk bonds fluctuated dramatically during the period covered, and the chance that a given bond will default increases rapidly over time.

Junk bond default losses are definitely rising. In 1989 4.04% of all junk bonds outstanding, worth $8.1 billion, defaulted. That performance compares with an average default rate of 3% over the previous five years and 2% for 1977 to 1978. Junk bond default rate increases mirror the decline in the quality of junk bond issuances. In 1980 the average junk bond company generated cash flow equal to 17% of debt, and earnings before interest, taxes, and depreciation at 2.73 times interest expense. By 1988 those ratios had deteriorated to 3% of debt and 1.23 times interest expense.

As Edward Altman, professor of the Stern School of Business at New York University, reported, BBB (lowest investment grade) bonds produced better returns than BB or B bonds in 1989 for the first time in ten years. In other words, the extra yield on junk bonds in 1989 no longer offset their extra risk. Altman noted that the 7% gap between junk and Treasury bonds implies that the market is anticipating sharply increased default rates of about 10% for 1990, assuming a 35% recovery on defaulted debt. As he reported, both Moody's and Standards & Poor's are predicting a 10% default rate, or $20 billion in total for 1990. He estimated that the default rate in 1990 will be well under that prediction, around 6%, making junk bonds an attractive investment.

Others disagree. Many expect more bloodshed as rising defaults crush confidence in junk bonds. The lack of secondary market liquidity and the refusal of the primary market to provide new financing are cited.

At this point, the debate over the merits of junk

bonds remains unresolved. But investors should be aware of the risks and how those risks can be minimized. About half of the junk bonds issued have resulted from leveraged buyouts and restructuring in which companies have swapped equity for debt. This debt is generally backed more by future cash flows than by tangible assets. This characteristic differentiates junk bond analysis from high-grade corporate bond analysis in that analyzing junk bonds is similar to analyzing common stock. As a result, junk bonds, like common stock, are more sensitive to the performance of the economy than they are to interest rates. A study by Salomon Brothers found that for the four years ending in 1988, junk bond prices were more correlated with the movements of the stock market than with the movement of bond market prices.

Another reason junk bonds are less sensitive to interest rate changes than are high-grade corporate bonds is that the higher coupon rates and shorter maturities provide a faster return of the investment to the buyer. A junk bond's value is determined less by distant interest and principal payments. As a result, a given interest rate change has less effect on the price of the bond.

Reducing Risk. Because 90% of all existing junk bonds have been issued since 1984, junk bonds have yet to be tested by a recession. Although the extent of the risk is debatable, we do know that it is substantial and that investors should plan to minimize it or at least reduce it. Diversification is the key to cutting risk to acceptable levels. A properly diversified portfolio should enable investors to generate returns sufficient to compensate for the risk in buying junk bonds. The best way for the individual investor to have a stake in a diversified portfolio of junk bonds is by purchasing mutual funds.

22

JUNK BOND
MUTUAL FUNDS

Individuals who invest in junk bonds should generally use mutual funds as the vehicle of choice. Mutual funds provide both professional management and the diversification of risk. Since junk bonds entail greater risk, diversification is crucial to obtaining the higher returns expected from junk bond investments. Few individuals have the capital and expertise to select an appropriate portfolio of at least 50 to 75 issues necessary to achieve proper diversification. Investors can buy mutual funds with as little as $500 to $1,000 and have an interest in a diversified portfolio.

Junk bond or "high-yield" mutual funds have grown dramatically in recent years along with the growth in the junk bond market. These funds are typically called "high yield" funds because of the stigma associated with the word "junk." Currently, there are 88 high-yield corporate bond funds with total assets of $28 billion.

The year 1989 was a debacle for junk bond mutual

funds producing a 1.5% downturn, making their three-year annual return (1987 to 1989) a rather dismal 3.9%. By contrast, high quality corporate bonds funds returned a solid 11.9% in 1989. As might be expected, investors in junk funds bailed out in droves. During 1989 redemptions of junk funds exceeded purchases by almost $2.9 billion. The legal and financial woes of Drexel Burnham Lambert and the publicized difficulties of big borrowers, such as Allied Stores, Federated Department Stores, and other junk bond issuers, crushed investor confidence in this market. Investors in the junk bond market should be aware of the possibility of a recession, which could produce an additional rash of junk bond defaults.

Yield vs. Total Return. Investors should be aware of the crucial distinction between yield and total return. One of the most common mistakes fund investors make is to shop for a bond fund by comparing yields. Instead, investors should focus upon total return, which includes not only dividends but also capital gains and losses. Investors do not increase their wealth when fat dividend checks fail to compensate for a plunge in the principal. Many junk bonds with 12 to 15% yields provided a negative total return in 1989 because of plunging bond prices. In selecting junk bond mutual funds, investors should evaluate the past perfomance of the fund by looking at the total return earned by the fund in the past.

Selecting Specific Funds. Investors should generally purchase no-load, high-yield junk bonds. Loads reduce the total amount being invested. For example, $10,000 invested in a 5% front-end fund results in a $500 sales charge and only a $9,500 investment in the fund. The load actually represents 5.3% of the net funds invested. Investors should remember that a load is a sales commission that accrues to whoever sells fund shares to an investor. A load does not go to the manager of the fund's assets nor does it serve as an incentive for the manager to perform better.

Investors should generally purchase open-end bond funds that continually issue new shares to sell to investors. These funds are the predominant form of mutual funds and are available directly from the fund or through a stockbroker. Closed-end funds do not issue new shares after their initial offering. Unlike open-end funds, they trade on one of the exchanges or over the counter. While open-end funds sell for their net asset value, closed-end funds are traded like common stock and can sell either at a premium or a discount from the portfolio's net asset value. Investors should not purchase closed-end funds when initially issued. Because so many of them trade at a discount from the market value of their portfolio, investors should wait to buy them in the secondary market.

Among the no-load, open-end, high-yield bonds that investors might consider are the following:

T. Rowe Price High Yield	(800) 638-5660
Vanguard High Yield Bond	(800) 662-7447
Fidelity High Income	(800) 544-6666

23

OVER-THE-COUNTER MARKET

After a corporate bond has been brought to market, it begins to trade in what is called the "secondary market." Bonds are originally issued in what is called the primary market. In the secondary market, bonds are traded among investors, both individual and institutional. Generally, buying or selling bonds in this market is a relatively simple procedure. Most corporate bonds, especially those issued by highly rated corporations, are readily marketable and are traded on exchanges or over-the-counter.

The secondary market encompasses both exchange and over-the-counter (OTC) trading. However, although some bonds are traded on the New York Stock Exchange, corporate bonds are primarily traded in the OTC market. Thus, the OTC market is the market of primary concern when bond trading is discussed.

The term over-the-counter originated when securities were traded over the counters in stores of various dealers from their inventory of securities. Currently, however, the term is a totally inaccurate description of how securities are traded in this market. Unlike the NYSE and the AMEX, the OTC market does not have centralized trading floors where all orders are processed. Instead, trading is conducted through a centralized computer-telephone network linking dealers across the country. These systems allow dealers to deal directly with one another and with customers.

The OTC market is thus a negotiated market where dealers buy and sell securities for their own account. The number of dealers that make a market in a particular security depends upon the popularity and the size of the issue. Each dealer making a market in a security purchases securities from sellers at a bid price while selling to buyers at a higher asked price. The difference between the bid and asked price is the spread, which represents the dealer's profit.

When an investor trades OTC, an order is presented to a broker. If the broker acts as a dealer in that security, the broker will fill the order from inventory. Otherwise, the broker will act as an agent in contacting the dealer who offers the best price. The broker usually charges a commission for finding the dealer who makes a market in the security.

Although the secondary market for corporate bonds is primarily in the dealer-made, over-the-counter market, a large number of bonds are traded on the New York Stock Exchange and a similar number on the American Stock Exchange. On both exchanges, a large proportion of listed bonds are convertible bonds. Institutions primarily confine their trading to the over-the-counter market. However, individual investors should generally stick to listed bonds. The market for most over-the-counter issues is not as liquid as the market for listed issues. A small sale order might cause the price of an inactively-traded bond to tumble.

Executing OTC Orders. Market orders and limit orders are the most common types of order executed by customers in the over-the-counter market. A market order must be transacted as quickly as possible and at the best price for the customer. A limit order designates the price at which the bond may be bought or sold. Limit orders, unless marked "good till canceled (GTC)," automatically become invalid if not executed by the close of trading that day. If marked GTC, the order remains valid until executed by the broker or canceled by the customer.

24

INVESTMENT BANKING

The primary market is the market in which new issues of bonds, preferred stock, or common stock are sold by companies to acquire new capital. In the primary market, the proceeds of sales go directly to the issuer of the securities that are sold. These new issues are typically of two types. The first type consists of seasoned new issues offered by companies with existing public markets for their securities. An example would be the issuance of additional bonds by IBM.

The second, smaller category is the issuance of new bonds by a small company selling bonds to the public for the first time. In this example, no public market for these bonds exists. This type of issue is typically referred to as an initial public offering.

The primary market should be distinguished from the secondary market, where previously issued securities are purchased and sold. Securities in the secondary market are bought and sold subsequent to original issuance. The proceeds of secondary market sales go to the selling dealers and investors and not to the companies that originally issued the securities.

Market for Corporate Bonds. Corporate bond issues can be brought to market initially either by public sale or private placement. In a public sale, a bond issue is offered in the open market to all interested buyers. In a private placement, the bonds are sold to a small number of investors. There are no public solicitations or bidding.

Public offerings of bonds are usually made through an investment bank, which acquires the total issue from the company and then sells the issue to interested investors. The relationship between the company and the underwriter can typically take three forms. The most common form occurs when an existing corporation negotiates with an investment bank, commonly one it has worked with on a continuous basis. When the firm decides to sell a new issue of corporate bonds, the investment bank advises the firm on the general characteristics of the issue, the price of the issue, and the timing of the offering.

Another arrangement occurs when the corporation announces that it desires to issue corporate bonds, and then solicits competitive bids from investment banking firms. Certain companies such as public utilities are required to submit their issues for competitive bids. Although such bidding can reduce the cost of the issue, some observers contend that it leads to a reduction in the quality of services provided by the investment bank.

The third type of arrangement occurs when the investment bank agrees to sell a new issue on a "best efforts" basis. This form is usually undertaken with speculative issues. The investment bank does not buy the issue but instead acts as a broker, selling the issue at a stipulated price. The commission on such an issue for the investment bank will be less than when the bank acquires the entire issue. However, there is less chance of a loss for the bank (see *Risk bearing,* below).

Functions of Investment Bankers. When bringing an issue to the primary market, an investment bank typically provides the client with four basic services:

1. *Advisement.* Initially, the investment bank will serve in an advisory capacity. When a firm decides to raise capital, the bank offers advice on the amount of money to borrow and the available means of raising it. Specifically, the investment bank will assist the issuer in making a determination as to the general characteristics of the issue and the price and timing of the offering. In addition, the investment bank may assist clients in analyzing mergers, acquisitions, and refinancing operations.

2. *Administration.* After the decision to issue the securities is made, the investment bank helps the client complete the paperwork and satisfy legal requirements. Of primary importance is the registration statement that must be filed with the Securities and Exchange Commission (SEC) before each interstate security offering. Registration is intended to ensure that adequate and accurate disclosure of material facts has been made concerning the company and the securities it proposes to sell.

Most of the information contained in the registration statement is also included in the prospectus that is prepared for public distribution. The prospectus must be distributed to every investor who is considering purchase of the new security. It contains information about the issuer's financial condition, management, business activities, planned use of the funds, and a detailed description of the securities to be issued.

3. *Risk bearing.* Investment banks generally agree to buy all of the new securities at a certain price. Then they resell these securities in smaller units to individual and institutional investors. This process is re-

ferred to as underwriting. The underwriting process involves risk because of the time interval between purchase by the investment bank and sale of the securities to investors. During this interval market conditions may deteriorate, forcing the investment bank to sell the securities at a loss.

If the issuance is too large for a single investment bank to handle alone, it can form a temporary partnership with other firms. Such a partnership is called a syndicate. The advantage of a syndicate is that it spreads the risk of loss over all of the investment banking firms in the group.

4. *Distribution.* The distribution service involves the marketing or sale of the securities after they have been purchased from the issuer. Once the syndicate receives the securities, members are allocated their portion of the securities to sell at a predetermined price. Investment bankers earn income by selling the security at a price that exceeds its cost—here, too, the difference is called the spread. The selling costs for common stock are much greater than those incurred for bonds. Bonds are sold in large blocks to a few large institutional investors, while common stock is usually sold to large numbers of individual stockholders.

Investment banks do not confine their activities to the primary market. They also play an important role in the secondary market. As dealers, investment banks buy and sell securities in which they specialize. Investment banks are also involved in trading large blocks of securities among institutional investors. Furthermore, they are involved in redistributing large blocks of securities to individuals and institutions through secondary offerings.

25

ACCRUED INTEREST

Bond interest payments are typically made semiannually on dates specified in the bond indenture. A bond indenture is a formal agreement between an issuer of bonds and the bondholders that includes provisions such as (1) form of the bond; (2) amount of the issue; (3) property pledged, if any; (4) protective covenants; (5) working capital and current rate requirements; and (6) redemption rights or call privileges. The indenture also includes an agreement providing for the appointment of a trustee to act on behalf of the bondholders.

When corporate bonds are issued on a date other than the interest payment date, buyers of the bonds will pay the seller the interest accrued from the last interest payment date to the date of issue. Then the purchaser will receive the full six months' interest payment on the next semiannual interest payment date. For example, assume XYZ Corporation issued bonds with par value of $1,000,000 and with 9% interest payable on January 1 and July 1. If these bonds were issued on March 1, the purchaser would have to pay the price of the bond plus the interest that had accrued since the last interest payment date (January 1). Assume the purchaser bought the entire issue at 98 on March 1. Since interest accrues at the rate of $90,000 a year or $7,500 a month, the purchaser would buy the bonds at 98% of $1,000,000—that is, $980,000 plus the accrued interest of $15,000 for a total of $995,000. The payment of $15,000 by the purchaser represents an advance payment enabling the purchaser to receive the full interest amount on the next payment date. As a result, on the next interest payment date (July 1) the purchaser will receive the usual semiannual interest payment of $45,000 ($1,000,000 \times .09 \times 6/12$) even though he/she has held the bonds for only four months.

Obviously, not all bonds are sold on dates that enable the computations to be as simple as the previous example. To calculate the exact amount of accrued interest, regardless of when the bond is purchased or sold, apply the following formula:

$$\frac{\text{Accrued}}{\text{Interest}} = \frac{\text{Annual}}{\text{Interest}} \times \frac{\text{Days in holding period}}{360 \text{ days}}$$

For corporate bonds, all whole months are assumed to have 30 days. To illustrate, let's take a sale by one individual to another. Assume bondholder John received his last interest payment of $60 on May 1. His next check is due on November 1. In July, he sells the bond to Jane for 98½ (or $985) for settlement on July 20. Ignoring commissions and fees, John has to pay Jane $985 plus an amount for accrued interest:

$$\frac{\text{Accrued}}{\text{Interest}} = \frac{\text{Annual}}{\text{Interest}} \times \frac{\text{Days in holding period}}{360 \text{ days}}$$

$$= (2 \times 60) \times \frac{(30 \text{ days} + 30 \text{ days} + 20 \text{ days})}{360 \text{ days}}$$

$$= 120 \times \frac{80 \text{ days}}{360 \text{ days}}$$

$$= \$26.67$$

The check that goes to John is for $1011.67 ($985 plus $26.67 accrued interest).

26

SETTLEMENT

The sale of a bond is completed by the transfer of title at the time payment is made. The actual transfer takes place on a settlement date required by industry rules even though the customer may pay the broker earlier. Delivery of the bonds from a seller's broker to the buyer's broker is required. However, automation has significantly reduced the number of actual deliveries of certificates.

When two investors enter into a secondary market bond transaction, they have to agree not only on the price but also on the date the actual exchange of bond certificates and cash will occur. Although different settlement options are available for other securities, all corporate bonds are traded the "regular way." A regular way trade calls for settlement five business days after the trade date. This requirement means that a trade entered into on Monday, June 14 will settle on Monday, June 21. (Weekends and holidays are not counted as business days.)

Although a customer's bonds may already be in possession of the broker, the exchange between the buying and selling sides will not take place for one calendar week. If the exchanges are closed for a holiday during the week, settlement is postponed for one additional day. If a trade is made on a Thursday before a holiday on Friday, settlement occurs on the following Friday.

Confirmations. Once a trade occurs, a confirmation is usually mailed to the customer on the business day following the trade day. A confirmation is a report describing the particulars of the order that has been executed. A typical confirmation will disclose the following:

1. Trade date
2. Settlement date
3. Security
4. Principal amount of bonds
5. Execution price
6. Commissions
7. Applicable taxes and fees
8. Money required (if any).

Customers should not assume that they do not have to pay the amount due before a confirmation notice is received in the mail. Regulation T of the Federal Reserve requires that a customer's funds be due in five business days, regardless of whether or not the customer received the confirmation.

The NYSE requires that a statement of account be sent to each customer every month in which the customer had account activity. When no such activity occurs, the customer must receive at least a quarterly statement. This statement summarizes the investment activity of the customer and gives dates for all entries such as trades, interest credited, deposits, and other activity.

27

REGISTERING
BONDS

Corporate bonds can be owned or registered in either the investor's name or the name of the brokerage firm (the "street name"). In the latter case the customer's name does not appear on the bond certificate or on the records of the transfer agent. In reality, the registered owner of the bonds is the brokerage firm acting as the agent of the customer. But the customer is not unprotected, as explained on the next page.

The first point is that in the case of bonds, the most common form of ownership is to have the certificates registered in the name of the investor. Several reasons account for most investors' preference for registering bonds in their own names. This procedure is routinely done for most purchases at no charge.

Interest checks are mailed directly to registered owners. When bonds are held in street name, the interest checks are sent to the brokerage firm first. Although brokerage firms mail interest checks to their customers promptly, customers whose bonds are held in street name may receive their interest checks several days or more than a week later than customers whose bonds are registered in their own names.

Registering certificates in the owner's name permits greater choice in selling the bonds. Such investors are not bound to a single broker and can choose the broker they want to sell the security. This choice also keeps brokers in the dark as to the investor's holdings. Some investors don't want commission-seeking brokers to be aware of the extent of their investments.

Street Name. Many investors prefer to have their certificates registered in street name. Active investors —those who buy and sell with some frequency— particularly desire this route because it simplifies the transfer process in the event of sale. No signature or certificate delivery is required of the customer when such certificates are sold.

In addition, because the broker holds the certificates, the customer does not have to worry about the certificates being lost or stolen. If the certificates in the owner's name are lost or stolen, the bonds cannot be sold until the certificates are replaced. Replacing certificates can be costly and time consuming.

Investors who keep their securities in a street name are protected up to $2 million if their broker belongs to the Securities Investors Protection Corporation (SIPC). It is important to check on a broker's coverage in this area before leaving any securities in a street name.

An investor who loses a bond certificate should immediately contact his or her broker. The broker will assist the customer in filing the necessary forms and determining the appropriate fees. Usually, the customer has to pay a fee of approximately 3% of the bond's value as a protection against the reappearance of the certificate at a later date. Although the bonds cannot be sold until the certificate is replaced (usually a period of several months), the customer will continue to receive scheduled interest payments. To diminish the chances of having bonds lost or stolen, investors should place their certificates in a safe deposit box.

28

SELECTING A BROKER

One way to enhance your long-term bond performance is to select a knowledgeable broker, also known as an account executive or registered representative. Although there are few brokers who deal exclusively in bonds, it is important to obtain a broker whose specialty is bond investing. A broker specializing in bond investments should be aware of new developments in the bond market and should be oriented to clients who are more interested in the income and safety of bond investments than in the growth potential of common stock.

Selecting a Firm. It is important to choose the appropriate brokerage firm. Start by asking your lawyer, accountant, or your friends for their opinion. Listen to their input, but don't accept advice without critically evaluating it. You can have more confidence in firms that are members of the New York Stock Exchange (NYSE), as they are subject to strict regulation and surveillance. To meet Exchange requirements, member firms must satisfy the following requirements:

1. Provide customers with their most recent financial statements.

2. Maintain a specified amount of capital at all times.
3. Undergo yearly audits by independent public accountants and be prepared for spot checks by Exchange examiners.
4. Submit to the Exchange up to 12 financial reports yearly.
5. Report to the Exchange details of certain borrowing or loans.
6. Carry fidelity insurance covering all of their employees and principals.

Selecting a Broker. Never invest with a broker by responding to a cold call or by purchasing securities after a single conversation. You, the investor, should take the initiative in selecting the broker. You should actively search for a broker who will meet your personal and financial needs.

Asking friends and associates their opinion is one way to find a good broker. Another way is to ask the office manager of a brokerage firm for his or her recommendation. The manager should know the capabilities of the various brokers in the firm and be able to refer you to a broker who is experienced and knowledgeable in selecting and trading bonds.

Once you have several candidates lined up, it is important to interview the candidates not only to determine their expertise in bonds, but also to see with whom you feel comfortable. Prepare for the interview by drawing up a list of questions to ask each candidate. This procedure enables you to compare the responses of the candidates to the same question. In setting up an interview time, select a period either before or after trading hours of the NYSE. Otherwise, your conversation may be interrupted repeatedly by the broker's current customers.

Some of the questions you might ask include:
1. What do you recommend that I do with the

money I have? (Watch out for the broker who recommends putting all your money in a high-risk investment.)
2. What is the broker's background? How long has he or she been trading bonds?
3. Ask about fees and commissions.
4. What return can you expect from your investment? (Be wary of brokers who make unrealistic promises.)
5. Where does the broker get investment ideas? (Does he/she give you the impression of confidence?)

Opening Your Account. Opening an account with a brokerage firm is a simple proposition. You'll be asked to provide your name, address, occupation, social security number, citizenship, and a suitable bank or financial reference. You also must prove that you are of legal age.

Two basic types of accounts exist: cash accounts and margin accounts. Most investors have "cash accounts," meaning that they settle transactions with cash. "Margin accounts" involve both cash and credit. These accounts are recommended only for experienced investors willing to assume the additional risk. In a margin account, you may buy bonds (or stocks) by paying only part of the cost, with the broker lending you the money to pay the remainder of the cost. If the bond price rises, the amount remaining after paying margin loan interest and commissions is your profit. If the bond price falls, you may have to deposit additional cash or securities to meet the margin maintenance requirements. The margin or percentage your broker can advance is set by the Federal Reserve Board.

As noted in the previous key, make sure that your account is covered by The Securities Investors Protection Corporation (SIPC).

29

BROKERS

Brokers can be divided into two groups: "full-service" brokers and "discount" brokers. Full-service brokers should provide information about the bonds you are considering for purchase. Many of these brokerage firms maintain research departments that investigate selected corporations and make recommendations for the account executives to pass on to their customers.

Discount brokers generally limit their service to executing orders for investors who know precisely what they want. Discount brokers cannot be counted on to provide advice or information. Because less service is provided to customers, the commissions or fees they charge are usually "discounted," or lower than those of full-service brokers.

Full-Service Brokers. A full-service broker should provide a wide range of services to customers, including investment research and advice. Although the research departments makes general recommendations, good brokers should offer suggestions to their clients based upon individual financial goals. In a full-service brokerage firm, there should be a personal relationship between the client and the account executive (who may also be called a registered representative or financial planner).

Brokers who work for full-service firms derive most of their income from a percentage of the commissions the firm charges the client.

Full-service brokers charge a commission or fee higher than that of a discount stockbroker. A typical fee for buying a bond from a full-service broker is $10 per $1000 face value; the fee for a discounter like Charles Schwab is $5 per $1000 face value. But bonds are not always sold on this basis. If the brokerage firm already owns the bond, the investor generally pays no commission, but is charged the difference between the bid and asked prices. This difference, called the spread, represents the broker's profit.

Full-service brokerage firms include such familiar names as Merrill Lynch, Dean Witter, Paine Webber, Prudential-Bache, and Shearson Lehman Hutton. These full-service brokers also offer advice on financial planning, cash management accounts, tax shelters, limited partnerships, and new issues of bonds.

Discount Brokers. For those investors who don't seek or want advice, discount brokers offer definite advantages. Customers should typically expect to save about 50% on their corporate bond commissions by using a discount broker. Discount brokers are able to offer these lower rates because they do not provide research; salaried order clerks handle the transactions rather than commissioned brokers, and they maintain low overhead.

The job of discount brokers is to execute transactions, not to persuade you to make a particular investment. Because full-service brokers earn their income from commissions, they have an incentive to encourage investors to make more trades. The more trades investors make, the more commission for the broker. Of course, most broker's make money over the long term by providing their customers with good advice and good service. But for some customers a big advantage of dealing with discount brokerage firms is that there are no sales calls.

Like full-service firms, discount firms will send investors monthly statements and confirmations of orders; such firms will also safeguard investors' certificates, maintain margin accounts and provide other services. Investors can thus place with discounters the same variety of orders: market orders (execute the trade at the best current price), limit orders (buy or sell at a specific price), and stop-loss orders (sell if the price drops below a certain value).

The over 100 discount brokerage firms provide varying levels of service. The largest is Charles Schwab, (800) 227-4444, which can sell investors stocks, options, over 300 mutual funds, corporate bonds, tax-exempt investments, Treasury securities, and CDs, and provides a money market fund where you can park your cash between other investments.

Other prominent discounters include:

Baker & Co.	(800) 321-1640
Pacific Brokerage Services	(800) 421-8395
Quick & Reilly	(800) 221-5220
Rose & Company	(800) 621-3700
Muriel Siebert & Co.	(212) 644-2400

30

SOURCES OF INFORMATION

Investors in bonds should not rely on bond ratings alone in making their decisions. Fortunately, there are various reliable sources of information useful to investors in making choices. One good source of information is the *Bond Guide* published by Standard & Poor's. A quick review of a *Bond Guide* can provide the following information:

1. Type of bond
2. Interest payment and maturity dates
3. Bond rating
4. Redemption provisions
5. Price trading ranges
6. Current yield and yield to maturity.

The *Bond Guide* provides a digest of relevant information on thousands of corporate and convertible bonds. You may be able to obtain a relatively recent copy from your broker. It can also be purchased directly from the publisher:

Standard & Poor's Corporation
25 Broadway
New York, NY 10004

Standard & Poor's (S & P) also publishes *Credit Week,* a weekly publication of news and analysis, and *Stock Reports,* which contain significant background information on more than 4000 public corporations including a 10-year record of income statement and balance sheet data. Finally, S & P also publishes a weekly, *The Outlook,* which frequently covers topics of interest to fixed-income investors.

When a potential bond investment is a new issue, a prospectus must be provided to bond buyers. The prospectus sets forth detailed information required by the Securities and Exchange Commission. Although reading a prospectus is the epitome of boredom, it is the best way to get detailed, useful information regarding the financial history of the issuing company, important data about the company's operations, and a description of the terms of the bond being issued.

The most widely read U.S. financial newspaper, *The Wall Street Journal,* has a page entitled Credit Markets, which is a useful source of information on the bond market. *Investor's Daily* is also a valuable source of information, particularly to those investors who use technical analysis in evaluating markets and making bond selections.

Barron's is a weekly financial newspaper and probably the best single source of data for technical analysis. A column called "Current Yield" is a particularly good source of information on the state of the bond market. *Barron's* is published by Dow Jones & Company, Inc., also the publisher of *The Wall Street Journal.* Subscription information on these publications can be obtained by writing:

The Wall Street Journal and/or Barron's
200 Burnett Road
Chicopee, MA 01021

Although *Business Week* and *Fortune* are excellent financial magazines, only *Forbes* provides a column that discusses bonds. This column, written by Ben Weberman, is an outstanding source of information about the bond market and individual bond issues. Weberman is extremely reliable and he makes specific recommendations that bond investors should consider. *Forbes* is published every two weeks and costs $48 a year. The subscriptions address is:

> *Forbes*
> 60 Fifth Avenue
> New York, NY 10011

31

RISK

Most investors would be classified as risk averse. They will only take on more risk if the expected return justifies the greater uncertainty. Although risk in general can be defined as the possibility of losing or not gaining value, there are many different kinds of risk.

Investors should be wary of any investment advertised as "risk free" or "riskless." In fact, every investment poses risk of one kind or another. Prudent investors understand the different types of risk and how to select investments that avoid or minimize the risks inherent in any investment.

Types of Bond Risk. Corporate bond investors are exposed to many of the same risks facing investors in other securities. Among the most important risks for bondholders are: (1) interest rate risk, (2) default risk, (3) business risk, (4) marketability risk, (5) inflation risk, and (6) event risk.

Interest rate risk is a function of change in bond prices caused by changes in interest rates. For investment-grade bonds (bond rating of BBB or higher), this is clearly the most important risk. Interest rates are set by market forces and constantly change as a result of such factors as changes in the money supply, capacity utilization, and the strength of the economy. The interest received by bondholders seldom changes because payments are fixed by contract. However, increases in general interest rates cause the prices of corporate bonds to decline, while a fall in rates precipitates an increase in bond prices.

Default risk is the possibility that a corporation will fail to make timely payments of interest and principal as they come due. Default risk is particularly prevalent when investments are made in lower-rated or junk bonds. Diversification is an important strategy for lessening but not eliminating this risk.

Investors in junk bonds should be aware of this risk. Since most junk bonds have been issued since the recession of 1981-1982, the danger of junk bonds in the face of a declining economy remains largely untested. Investors should carefully evaluate the financial viability of a firm issuing junk bonds.

Business risk is the risk of falling bond prices caused by the declining economic fortunes of the company. Business risk has a greater impact on junk bonds than interest rate risk. Since companies issuing junk bonds often do not have sufficient assets to cover their obligations, investors are dependent upon rising earnings and, particularly, increased cash flow to meet debt interest and principal. Issuers of investment-grade bonds typically have a much stronger capacity to pay principal and interest, thus significantly reducing the business risk associated with these bonds.

Marketability risk relates to the liquidity of the obligation and the ease with which a bond issue can be sold at the prevailing market price. Marketability risk is another risk that is associated with junk bonds. Many such issues scarcely change hands after the initial offering; some go for months without trading. Therefore, the latest traded price may not be indicative of the current market price. Many observers see a real danger for lower-quality bonds if investors become net sellers but no buyers come forward until an extremely low price has been attained. The marketability risk is another factor that argues for investing in junk bonds only through high-yield mutual funds with well-diversified portfolios.

Inflation risk is based on the virtual certainty that there will continue to be increases in the general level of prices. Bond investors only realize a real return if their return exceeds the rate of inflation. Because most bonds pay a fixed coupon rate of interest that may not keep pace with inflation, bond investments are vulnerable to inflation risk. In the 1960s and 1970s, corporate bonds actually realized a real negative return (return less than the rate of inflation). Current coupon rates on corporate bonds are higher than those of the 1960s and 1970s, reflecting a more realistic view of inflation risk.

Event risk is the risk of a takeover, leveraged buyout, or restructuring that reduces the perceived quality, and therefore price of the existing outstanding bonds. For example, the leveraged buyout of RJR Nabisco by Kohlberg Kravis Roberts & Co. (KKR) reduced the price of its corporate bonds by about 20% in one week. Since these deals are financed with the issuance of large amounts of additional debt, the financial position of the firm deteriorates, frequently converting existing bonds into junk bonds. Corporate bondholders are now forcing new issuances of bonds to contain covenants that provide protection against event risk. Investors who are interested in buying seasoned issues in the secondary market but are concerned with event risk can purchase bonds of companies such as public utilities, which are relatively free of this risk. (However, beware of utilities bogged down in struggles to open nuclear power plants.)

32

DETERMINANTS OF DISCOUNTS OR PREMIUMS

Bonds are considered fixed-income securities because the debt-service obligations of the issuer are fixed. Accordingly, the issuer agrees to (1) repay a fixed amount of principal at the maturity date and (2) pay a fixed amount of periodic interest to the owner of record. Normally, interest is payable every six months. The principal due at maturity is called the par or face value—usually $1,000 per bond.

Bond prices are quoted as a percentage of par value. Thus, a bond selling at 101 means that it sells at 101% of $1,000 par, or $1,010. Any examination of bond quotes shows that bond prices seldom sell at their par value. Some sell at a price less than par; these are called discount bonds. Others sell at a price exceeding par; these are called premium bonds. The discount or premium is measured by the difference between a bond's current market price and its par value.

Determinants. Why do bonds sell at a discount or premium? The rate of interest actually earned by bondholders is called the yield. If bonds sell at a discount, the yield is higher than the coupon rate. Conversely, if bonds sell at a premium, the yield is lower than the coupon rate.

Bonds sell below par when investors demand a rate of interest or yield higher than the coupon rate. The investors are dissatisfied with the coupon rate because they can earn a greater interest rate on alternative investments of equal risk. The lack of demand for the bond at par value forces the price of the bond down to where its yield is more or less equivalent to alternative investments of equal risk.

Conversely, bonds sell above par when investors are satisfied with a yield that is lower than the coupon rate. In other words, alternative bonds of equal risk provide a yield less than the coupon rate specified in the bond. Under these conditions, investors will bid up the price of the bond to where its yield corresponds to other bonds of similar characteristics and risk.

Another factor determining the discount or premium on a bond is the quality of the bond issuer. This quality is best indicated by its bond rating, although there is often a lag between changes in the economic fortunes of a firm and changes in its bond rating. The takeover binge of the 1980s has raised questions about the quality of many bond issuers. Many firms have seen their investment-grade bonds converted to junk bonds as corporate raiders have piled on debt to finance these takeovers. The reduction in quality as evidenced by a deteriorating economic position has been followed by declining corporate bond prices and increased discounts.

Proximity to the maturity date is an additional factor affecting discounts and premiums. Bonds typically have a fixed maturity date—the date the principal is to be repaid. The closer a bond is to its maturity date, the closer its price should be to par (price received at maturity). The further a bond is from its maturity date, the greater the probability of it selling at a large discount or premium. But new issues often trade at or close to par because their interest rates have been set according to the market.

Finally, call features influence the amount of discount or premium. A bond that is callable can be redeemed prior to its maturity date. Bonds are usually not callable for the first five or ten years after they are issued. The bond is said to have call protection during this period. Once the call protection has expired, the bond may become callable either at any time or only on certain dates. The bond's indenture will specify the terms.

When a bond is called, the issuer generally has to pay a small premium over par to compensate the investor for the inconvenience. However, as time passes, most callable bonds become callable at progressively lower prices until, eventually, they are callable at par. Generally, bonds approaching their call date will not sell at a significant difference from call price. Typically, it is assumed that corporations will call the bonds if it is to their advantage to do so (that is, if prevailing interest rates are significantly less than the coupon rate; see Key 33).

33

BOND INDENTURE

The bond indenture is a legal document between the issuer and the bondholder specifying the legal conditions that must be met by the issuer and the rights of the bondholders. For all corporate bonds issued in interstate commerce with a total price exceeding $5 million, the Trust Indentures Act requires that a trustee be appointed. The trustee, usually a bank, is responsible for protecting the rights of the bondholders and determining that all the indenture provisions are met, including the timely payment of interest and principal. Although a bond indenture contains many protective covenants of little interest, investors should be aware of several significant provisions.

Callable Bonds. Many corporate debt securities are callable bonds, allowing the issuer the right to retire the bonds at a certain price stipulated in the bond contract. Typically, issuers have an incentive to call in their existing bonds if the current interest rate is lower than the coupon rate being paid on the bond.

Three types of call provisions exist:

1. The bond is freely callable, which means the issuer can retire the bond at any time after a notification period of usually 30-60 days.
2. The bond is noncallable, which means the bond cannot be retired prior to its maturity.
3. The bond has a deferred call feature, which means that the bond cannot be called for a certain length of time after the date of issue. At the end of the deferred call period the bond becomes freely callable. The most common deferred call period is between five and ten years. If the issuer of the bonds exercises the option to call bonds, the bondholder is usually paid a penalty or premium over par for the inconvenience.

To enhance investor interest in its bonds, a corporate issuer may adopt several features to make the security more marketable. One such feature is a sinking fund provision. In a *sinking fund,* funds are set aside for the orderly retirement of bonds prior to the maturity date. Sinking funds offer additional protection to the bondholders. Consequently, the yields on bonds secured by sinking funds are lower than those of bonds without such funds.

Another feature adopted to make bonds more attractive to investors is *convertibility.* Convertible bonds allow holders the option of surrendering the bonds and receiving in return a specified number of shares of common stock. The conversion feature gives bondholders the opportunity to take advantage of rising stock prices. Because of this option, convertible bonds yield less than comparable bonds not providing convertibility (see Key 11).

Recent Developments. The recent takeover binge has made corporate bondholders wary. These takeovers are financed by a great deal of debt, which tends to make the previously outstanding bonds riskier, thus decreasing their quality. To allay investor fears, many issuers have incorporated new safeguards in the bond indenture.

Known on Wall Street as "poison puts," the covenants protect investors in the event of takeover by requiring that the existing bonds be retired at par or face value or at a slight premium over par. This covenant is usually triggered if a large portion of a company's stock is purchased by one buyer and the bond ratings are downgraded. In return for easing the fears of investors, poison puts enable issuers to sell bonds at a lower interest rate.

In 1989, Standard & Poor's Corporation started grading the protection offered in individual covenants on a 1–4 scale. Moody's Investors Service says that it evaluates puts in setting overall company ratings. Initially, puts were part of debt issued by less creditworthy companies. Lately, however, puts are being included in investment-grade bonds.

34

BONDS WITH WARRANTS

Warrants are options to buy a fixed number of shares of common stock at a predetermined price during a specified time period. They are sometimes issued by corporations as attachments to a new issue of corporate bonds. The warrants are used by companies as inducements to make the new issue easier to sell. Warrants are often issued by corporations that are having financial problems and anticipate some difficulty in selling a new issue of corporate bonds to raise capital.

Example of Warrants. Warrants are typically detachable from the bond to which they were attached when issued. Subsequently, they trade on the exchanges or over the counter, like the bonds to which they were attached. When issued, the price at which the warrant can be exercised is fixed above the current market price of the stock. For example, a warrant may entitle the holder to the right to buy one share of XYZ Corporation at 14 when the common stock is current-

105

ly trading at 10. The warrant is theoretically worthless since the exercise price is greater than the market price. However, the warrant will have speculative value and trade at a price that reflects characteristics of the stock and warrant. Assume the warrant currently trades at $1. Suppose the stock doubles from $10 to $20, producing a 100% gain for holders of the common stock. What happens to the price of the warrant? In this case, the warrant will trade at a price of at least $6, producing a 600% gain.

But leverage works both ways. If the price of the stock drops to $5, the investor has a 50% loss on the holdings of common stock. However, if the term to maturity expires, the warrant is worthless, producing a 100% loss. Warrant prices go up or down faster than the prices of the underlying stock.

Valuation of Warrants. The price of a warrant can be divided into two components: (1) the intrinsic value and (2) the speculative value. The intrinsic value of a warrant is the market price per share of stock less the exercise price per share, multiplied by the number of shares of common stock obtained with one warrant. This calculation determines the intrinsic value assuming the market price exceeds the exercise price of the warrant. If the warrant price exceeds the market price, the intrinsic value of the warrant is zero. For example, assume a warrant entitles its holder to buy two shares of stock at an exercise price of $25 when the market price is $30. In this case, the warrant has an intrinsic value of $10 [($30 − $25) × 2].

In addition, a warrant has speculative value. Speculative value is determined predominantly by the following combination of factors:

1. *The potential leverage of the warrant that is dependent upon the ratio of the stock price to the warrant price.* The greater the potential leverage, the higher the speculative value (the

106

higher the warrant price).

2. *The price volatility of the underlying stock.* Volatile stocks move up and down faster. The greater the volatility of the underlying stock, the greater the speculative value of the warrant.

3. *The time to maturity.* The longer the time to maturity, the greater the speculative value.

4. *The dividend paid by the stock.* The larger the dividend, the smaller the premium. The holders of warrants are not entitled to receive dividends.

Conclusion. The sale or exercise of warrants does not affect the status of the bond. The bond continues to pay interest and principal even if the warrant is sold or converted into common stock. Warrants usually have a ten-year life span. Typically, the warrants are not effective until a set period after issuance of the corporate bond. For example, a 20-year bond with warrants might be issued in 1990 with a warrant exercisable between 1995 and 2005 and final maturity in 2010. Between 2005 and 2110, the bonds will sell "ex-warrants."

Investors should not ignore the value of warrants attached to corporate bonds. If the stock price rises substantially, the warrants may prove to be of considerable investment value. Investors should periodically monitor the price of warrants with the bonds by checking with their broker.

35

BOND SWAPS

A bond swap is simply the sale of one bond issue and the purchase of another. The purpose of bond swaps is to increase either current or expected future yield on the money invested. A bond swap is designed to take advantage of the relative changes in yield between two different bonds. The difference in yield between one bond and another bond is called the spread. The spread between two bonds may change because bonds with different characteristics are influenced differently as investment conditions change. For example, a declining interest rate might push up the price of one bond more than another because of the difference in its provisions.

Although the subject of bond swaps can be extremely complicated, the individual investor need only be concerned with the principal types. Because transaction costs are proportionately higher on small trades than on larger ones, most swaps are not appropriate for the small investor. The four principal types of bond swaps are: (1) substitution swaps, (2) intermarket spread swaps, (3) rate anticipation swaps, and (4) tax swaps.

A *substitution swap* is one in which the investor increases yield by swapping one bond for another almost identical bond that yields slightly more. For example, an investor might sell a 20-year 10% bond selling at face value ($1000) and purchase a 20-year 10% bond selling for $980. This swap increases the investor's current yield by 20 basis points ($100/$980 = 0.1020). This strategy is not very useful for the small investor because the transaction costs involved make the swap unprofitable.

Intermarket spread swaps (also called yield spread swaps) exploit the spread in different markets such as government bonds versus corporate bonds. An investor making this swap is gambling that the relationship between two yields will narrow or widen over time. The yield spread between government bonds and corporate bonds may change in response to new developments. If the investor's forecast of future yield spreads is incorrect, however, there is the real risk of capital loss.

For example, an investor might swap a bond with a lower yield in one market for a bond with a higher yield in another. If the price of the higher-yielding bond rises or the price of the lower-yielding bond falls, or both, the spread narrows and the investor profits from the transaction.

Rate anticipation swaps are for those investors who feel they can anticipate interest rate swings. Assume an investor projects a substantial decline in interest rates. An appropriate strategy would be to switch from short-term to long-term bonds, since long-term bonds would appreciate more than short-term bonds in a period of declining interest rates. Another strategy in the face of declining interest rates would be for an investor to swap long-term premium bonds for long-term discount bonds. Bonds that sell at a premium are less volatile than discount bonds. Therefore, owners of discount bonds should generate a greater capital gain than owners of premium bonds.

A final swap is what can be called a *tax swap*. These are frequently advertised at year-end by brokerage firms as a strategy for reducing taxes. This strategy works best when interest rates are at relatively high levels. At these levels, many bonds are selling below face value and their original owners usually have paper losses (current price is less than the issuance price). A tax swap involves the sale of bonds whose current price is less than their initial cost in order to establish a tax loss. The money received is then reinvested in a similar bond. The loss realized from the sale of bonds can be used to reduce ordinary income of up to $3000 or used to reduce a capital gain (in any amount) from the sale of another security during the taxable year. If the loss is greater than $3000, it can be carried over into the next year.

For example, assume that an investor owns an issue of bonds that has a 6% coupon rate, a maturity of 20 years, and an AA bond rating. Assume further that these bonds have declined in value from $10,000 to $7000. If these bonds are sold for $7000 and the money is used to purchase bonds with the same terms, the investor will realize a loss of $3000—but his/her portfolio will remain virtually unchanged. A tax swap enables investors to maintain their position by buying comparable bonds selling for approximately the same price.

36

BUYING NEW ISSUES

There are essentially two sources of bonds to the investor: the new-issue market and the secondary market. The latter market trades bonds after they have been issued. The principal secondary market for corporate bonds is an over-the-counter market (see Key 37). The distribution of new issues is covered by rules established by the Securities and Exchange Commission.

One approach to obtaining information about new issues is to watch announcements, called tombstones, printed in *The Wall Street Journal* and in other major financial publications. These give basic details about the issue and list the underwriting group members involved in the offering. This approach may lead to disappointment, however, because corporate issues are often presold. Even if the bonds have been presold, the tombstone announcements are required by the SEC.

Another source of information is the weekly publications describing proposed offerings. Both *Moody's Bond Survey* and *Creditwatch,* published by Standard & Poor's, provide summary information about proposed offerings. Some of the details provided include the business of the issuer, use for the proceeds, bond rating, security for the bonds, guarantees, call provisions, and statistical highlights about the issuer. Both of these publications can usually be found at local libraries.

The best source of information about new bond issues is to have a knowledgeable account executive (AE). A good AE should be able to alert an investor to a new bond issue that satisfies his/her objectives. Finding such an AE is not necessarily simple. Because of low trading volume and low commissions, most AEs are not that informed about bonds. To find such an individual, select a firm that has extensive retail operations and is active as an underwriter and dealer in corporate bonds. Then call the office manager and ask him for an experienced AE in trading corporate bonds.

Once you have selected an AE, he/she should be able to suggest a new issue to satisfy your objectives even before it is announced in the newspapers. Although the exact terms such as the coupon rate will not be known yet, he/she can supply you with an estimate and a copy of a preliminary prospectus, also called a "red herring." This document provides detailed information about the issuer's financial background and a description of the particular type of bond to be issued. The terms of the bond do not appear in the preliminary prospectus. However, the information presented is usually sufficient to determine whether an investor is interested in placing a reservation for the bonds.

For attractive issues, bond reservations should be made as soon as possible for these issues are usually sold in the order reservations are received. Such reservations are always conditional. The reservation is usually made on the basis of an estimated coupon rate or within specified limits of the estimate. If the announced terms are less than what was specified in the reservation, the AE must call the investor to see if he/she can proceed with the order.

Advantages of New Issues. New issues have certain advantages that appeal to many investors. First, no commission is charged the buyer of a new issue. The bond issuer pays the commission.

New bonds are typically issued with little or no accrued interest. Accrued interest is the interest that has accumulated between the most recent payment date and the sale of a bond. At the time of sale, the buyer pays the seller the bond's price plus the accrued interest. Many investors wish to avoid paying accrued interest when purchasing bonds because it is money that is not returned until the next interest payment date.

Finally, new issues are typically going to sell at or near face value ($1000). Many investors prefer to purchase bonds at a price which approximates face value in order to have the additional bonds priced in $1000 increments. Zero-coupon bonds are an exception because they are priced at a substantial discount from face value.

37

SECONDARY MARKET

Sales of new issues take place in what is called the primary market (see Key 36). In the primary market, proceeds of sales go to the issuer of securities. After new issues have been sold, trading takes place in what is called the secondary market. The secondary market includes exchanges and the over-the-counter market where securities are bought and sold after their original issuance. The proceeds of secondary market sales belong to selling dealers and investors, not to the companies that originally sold the securities.

The principal secondary market for corporate bonds is the over-the-counter market. Currently, the overwhelming majority (in excess of 90%) are traded over the counter and only a small portion of the total trading volume takes place on the exchanges. Bonds traded on the exchanges are called listed bonds in contrast to unlisted securities which are traded in the over-the-counter market.

The New York Stock Exchange (NYSE) is by far the largest bond market of any exchange. Over 90% of the listed bonds appear on the NYSE, with the remainder listed on the American Stock Exchange and a few regional exchanges. The NYSE offers investors a broad selection of about 4000 bonds with an aggregate face value of more than $300 billion. NYSE bond prices are listed daily in newspapers such as *The Wall Street Journal* and *Investor's Daily,* and weekly in

Barron's. Generally, trading on the exchanges is in small lots while the overwhelming majority of bonds are traded over the counter in large (100 to 1000 lots) blocks between institutional investors. The "rule of 10" on the NYSE requires members to execute customers' orders for nine bonds or fewer on the floor of the exchange unless a better price can be received elsewhere. Most bond trading at the NYSE takes place through the Automated Bond System (ABS), a sophisticated electronic system enabling brokers to transmit their customers' orders to the NYSE for almost instant execution.

The secondary market provides investors much greater choice than buying bonds on the primary market. As noted, a large number of bonds are listed on the exchange and many more are traded in the over-the-counter market. Meanwhile, the number of new issues that become available each month might be 20 to 40 issues, and only a few of these might meet the investor's objectives.

The secondary market also enables the investor to purchase some attractive bonds selling at a discount (less than their par or face value). Discounted bonds usually have been issued during a prior period when interest rates were lower. When held to maturity, discounted bonds guarantee capital gains. In periods when higher yields prevail, previously issued bonds with lower coupon rates have their prices adjusted downward to reflect the increasing coupon rates which are available in new-issue bonds. During these periods, investment-grade bonds can be selling for as much as $200-$400 below face value. These bonds will appreciate back to their face value at maturity, or even sooner if interest rates decline sufficiently.

Discounted bonds are best purchased when interest rates peak and begin their downward cycle. Investors who anticipate declining interest rates should purchase long-maturity, low-coupon discount bonds. The longer the maturity, the greater the profit that accrues to the investor. The lower the coupon rate, the greater the percentage of capital gains to be realized. Alternatively, when interest rates are climbing, the best strategy is to buy short-maturity, high-coupon bonds.

Advantages of Listed Bonds. For small investors, it is usually wise to stick to listed bonds. The most important reason is improved marketability. These bonds are usually more actively traded than many unlisted bonds and brokerage offices can furnish a reliable quote on listed bonds. Unlisted bond quotes may vary widely from dealer to dealer.

Bonds are quoted in terms of bid and asked prices. A typical quote might be 93-96, 30 up. This quote is interpreted as follows:

Available for sale: 30 bonds with face value of $30,000 at an asked price of 96 ($28,800)

Desire to purchase: 30 bonds with face value of $30,000 for a bid price of 93 ($27,900).

The difference between the bid and asked prices (spread) represents profits to the dealer. Larger issues tend to have more market makers and a narrower spread. Smaller issues may be infrequently traded and have spreads of 5 or 6 points.

Prices on over-the-counter issues that are not actively traded can drop several points with only the sale of five bonds. Thus, the seller who buys unlisted bonds often faces a relatively illiquid market. When purchasing new issues, investors can determine whether the bond issuer intends to apply for listing. Issuers typically apply and pay for listing before a new issue is offered for sale.

When buying bonds that are infrequently traded, investors should place limit orders. Limit orders are orders to buy or sell a bond at a specific price or better. This order contrasts with market orders where the security is bought or sold at the best available price.

38

THE SECURITIES
AND EXCHANGE
COMMISSION

Prior to the Great Depression of the 1930s, the federal government did little to regulate the securities markets. However, the depression resulted in the widespread collapse of the securities markets, fostering criticism of their operation. In an effort to restore confidence in their operation, Congress intervened and established the Securities and Exchange Commission (SEC) to administer federal laws that seek to provide protection for investors. The overriding purpose of these laws is to ensure the integrity of the securities markets by requiring full and fair disclosure of material facts related to securities offered to the public for sale. In addition, the SEC is empowered to initiate litigation in instances of fraud.

Securities Act of 1933. The Securities Act of 1933 provides for the regulation of the initial public distribution of a corporation's securities and for full and fair disclosure of relevant information concerning such issues to prospective purchasers. Various civil and criminal penalties are applicable to those who misrepresent information required to be disclosed under this act. Under the provisions of this act, new issues sold publicly through the mails or in interstate commerce must be registered with the SEC. The SEC has special forms that must be completed that require disclosure of information such as:

1. Description of the registrant's properties and business
2. Description of significant provisions of the security to be offered for sale and its relationship to the registrant's other capital securities
3. Information about the management of the registrant
4. Financial statements certified by independent public accountants.

After the registration statement is filed, it becomes effective on the twentieth day after filing unless the SEC requires amendments. During this period it is unlawful for the securities to be sold. Registration statements are examined for compliance with applicable statutes and regulations. Moreover, if the SEC discovers that the registration statement is materially misleading, inaccurate, or incomplete, it can prohibit the securities from being sold to the public.

The SEC does not insure investors from losses. Nor does it prevent the sale of securities in risky, poorly managed, or unprofitable companies. Rather, registration with the SEC is designed to provide adequate and accurate disclosure of required material facts about the company and securities it proposes to sell.

A portion of the information contained in the registration statement is included in a prospectus that is prepared for public distribution. Every investor must be provided with a prospectus. The prospectus includes audited financial statements, information about the firm's history, large stockholders, and other relevant facts.

When a bond is a new issue, regulations of the SEC permit underwriters to furnish a preliminary prospectus. This document furnishes information describing a firm's financial history but it does not contain all the information that will appear in the final prospectus including the offering price and coupon rate. The purpose of a preliminary prospectus is to gauge the interest of investors in the issue. The preliminary prospectus is also called a red herring because portions of the cover page are printed in red ink.

39

SOME DO'S AND DON'T'S

Do's

1. Do some research before purchasing a bond. Don't just take the advice of your broker. Consult Standard & Poor's *Bond Guide* for pertinent information on the bond. Your broker should have it, or check with a local library. Familiarize yourself with some of the useful publications cited in Key 30.

2. Make certain that you understand the terms of the bond before making the purchase. If you don't understand something, consult your broker or the issuer.

3. Determine that the bond is the appropriate investment for you in terms of risk, return, and term to maturity. Be objective about your tolerance for risk. If your tolerance is low, sacrifice some return. You should be comfortable with your investment.

4. Check the bond rating. If you are uncomfortable taking risks, select only those bonds whose rating is "A" or above.

5. If you decide to buy lower-rated bonds or junk bonds because of the higher return, diversification is essential. Diversification is the key to

reducing risk. Although junk bonds can on average exceed the return on Treasury issues by as much as 5-7%, the risk is much greater. Moody's found that 17.4% of junk bonds issued in 1979 defaulted over a ten-year period ending in 1989. It would be no surprise if this rate increased in the future.

6. Most investors buying junk bonds should purchase high-yield junk bond funds with at least 75-100 issues in their portfolio. In this way, you get professional management and diversification of risk.

7. Keep up with your investments. At a minimum, read the financial section of a good newspaper.

Don't's

1. Don't act on tips. Get your own information.

2. Don't assume that bonds involve no risk. Bond prices are subject to risk just like other investments. Be aware of the risks and act to minimize them.

3. Don't buy investments that make you nervous. You should always be comfortable with your investments. If they make you uneasy, your investment program needs to be revised. Select alternative investments that better suit your needs.

4. Do not buy junk bonds unless you understand the risks involved. Remember that economic performance may have an even greater impact on junk bond prices than interest rates. The junk bond market has grown dramatically since the last recession ending in 1982. How junk bond prices will fare in the next recession is highly uncertain.

5. Don't put all your eggs in one basket. Always diversify your risks. This is a key difference between investing and gambling.

40

ASSET ALLOCATION

Before beginning an investment program, every investor should map out his or her own financial profile. A wise investor must begin with self analysis. Certain questions need to be answered before an investment program can be worked out: What are my objectives and goals? What is my net worth? How much risk am I willing to assume? What are my debts and moral obligations?

Perhaps the first step in any investment program is to identify your goals and objectives. Every investor should be aware of what he or she is trying to accomplish by investing. These goals need to be written down and referred to when setting up your investment program. Your goals should be divided into immediate or near-term (within the next several years) and long-range goals.

Before making any investment, you must know your net worth. This process enables you to match your investments to your resources and to accomplish your financial goals. The calculation is simple. Add up everything you own—the total is your assets. Subtract from your total assets the value of everything you owe (your liabilities). The difference between your total assets and your total liabilities is your net worth.

The concept of risk is often overlooked when the returns from various investments are cited. As a general rule, the more risk you assume, the higher the potential reward. Your net worth and your potential income are factors in dictating the amount of risk you can assume. Of further importance is the psychological aspect of assuming risk. No investment should be entered into if it causes anxiety and loss of sleep.

Before making any investment, you should examine the adequacy of your life insurance and disability coverage and establish an emergency fund. An emergency fund consists of bank savings or money market funds that are available to meet unexpected needs. An investor should plan on the possibility of paying unexpected expenses without having to liquidate long-term investments.

Asset Allocation. In his book *Asset Allocation: Balancing Financial Risk* (Dow Jones-Irwin), Roger Gibson says, "Successful investing has very little to do with complicated tasks like picking the right individual stocks or calling market turns." Gibson contends that the most important decision in investing is how you divide your money between stocks, bonds, and cash. For support he cites a study in the July-August 1986 issue of *Financial Analysts Journal,* which evaluates the ten-year performance of 91 pension funds. The study concludes that 94% of the funds' returns were due to the way investments were allocated, while only 6% resulted from market timing and from specific picks within each asset group.

In the past, common stocks have been the best long-term investment. However, common stocks entail substantial risk. They can go down or up substantially. Investors should not be misled by the booming stock market of the 1980s when stocks (measured by

123

Standard & Poor's 500 Index) went up an average of 17% a year. This period was one of the great bull markets in stock market history. The likelihood of it being repeated over the next ten years is not high. There have been substantial periods of time when it has been very difficult to make money investing in common stocks. For example, over the period from 1966 to 1982, the returns from common stocks were actually negative after adjusting for inflation.

Investors should remember one of Wall Street's oldest rules: diversification reduces risk. Well-diversified portfolios containing stocks, bonds, cash, or money funds can reduce volatility in investment returns. Even better, volatility can be reduced with only a small reduction in potential return. The best investment over the period from 1970 to 1989 was common stock, which returned an average of 11.5%. Meanwhile, corporate bonds returned about 9% over the same period. However, for the investor with a diversified portfolio, risk was reduced with only a minor sacrifice in returns. A portfolio of 60% stocks and 40% bonds would have returned slightly less than 11% over this period.

Although common stocks have been the best long-run capital investment, investment in corporate bonds can have advantages over investment in common stocks. For those investors who desire to protect their principal and establish a steady stream of income, corporate bonds are the answer. Those investors who want to maximize current income should remember that corporate bonds generate greater current income than CDs, money market funds, government bonds, and stocks. Finally, corporate bonds offer greater security in the receipt of income than most common stocks, since interest on a corporate bond must be paid before dividends on common or preferred stock of the same corporation are paid.

On the other hand, no investor should have his

entire portfolio consist of bonds (corporate or governmental). Although bonds are viewed as much less volatile than stocks, over the last decade bonds have been nearly as risky as stocks. Shearson Lehman Hutton's index of U.S. government and corporate bonds has produced returns ranging from as little as 2.29% in 1987 to as much as 31.09% in 1982.

Although the composition of your portfolio should reflect your risk tolerance, liquidity needs, tax status, holding period, and income requirements, a reasonable mix of assets for aggressive investors would be 60% of your portfolio invested in stocks, 30% in bonds, and 10% in cash. This mix of assets would have provided an investor an average return of about 9.5% since 1965.

The cash position should include such investments as short-term CDs, Treasury bills, and money market funds, all of which are highly liquid, almost riskless investments. In buying both bonds and stocks, diversification is important and requires at least 10 to 15 different bonds and the same number of stocks in diverse industries. An investor who cannot afford this level of diversification should invest in stocks and bonds through the purchase of no-load mutual funds.

41

BUYING CORPORATE BONDS

Bonds have traditionally been regarded as safe investments, most suitable for conservative investors. Until about 1970, volatility in the bond market was much lower than in the stock market, and investors felt confident that they could purchase bonds and store them away. The simpler times are gone. Bonds have become much more volatile, moving more in one week than they did in a year 30 years ago.

New dangers prey on bond investors. Bonds may be retired prematurely (called), forcing the investor to reinvest funds at lower interest rates. In addition, a leveraged buyout or restructuring, which results in loading debt on the corporate balance sheet, can cause bond prices to plummet.

Buying bonds is no longer a one-decision process. Investors have to be prepared to sell the bonds if conditions change. What are the main risks investors have to consider? Two risks apply to all corporate bonds.

A rise in interest rates decreases the value of all corporate bonds. This risk requires the investor to watch for trends in interest rates.

The other concern is the specific risk associated with changes in the financial condition of the company. A decline in the creditworthiness of the corporation increases the chance that it will default and pushes down the price of the bond. This risk has particularly devastated the value of junk bond holdings recently.

Timing Purchases and Sales. The best time to buy corporate bonds is before a recession, when prevailing interest rates will drop because of falling demand for credit. This strategy works even better if the recession is unexpected and bond prices have not anticipated declining interest rates. The best time to sell bonds is before an inflationary period, when interest rates soar because of greater demand for money. Again, this strategy succeeds better if you sell when interest rates have not anticipated the increase in inflation.

Since the most important single determinant of bond prices is interest rates, smart investors anticipate interest rates in purchasing and selling bonds. For example, if interest rates are expected to rise, they shorten their maturities (long-term bonds decline more than short-term bonds when interest rates rise). If interest rates are expected to sink, they lengthen their maturities to lock in the current high yields for future years and profit accordingly from the rising bond prices that accompany falling rates.

Investors should not be confident of their ability to forecast interest rate trends. The news media is bombarded on a daily basis with conflicting advice from economists, money managers, and financial planners on future interest rate levels. Many experts maintain that investors should not even attempt to predict interest rate turns. What is the individual investor to do? While there is no magic formula for predicting future interest rates, there are several indicators investors can follow:

1. *Maturities of Money Market Funds.* William Donoghue, in *The Donoghue Strategies* (Bantam Books, 1989), has found the average maturity of taxable money funds to be an extremely useful warning signal of higher rates. Money market funds invest in Treasury bills, bank certificates of deposit, and other short-term securities. His indicator reflects the decisions of more than 500 of the nation's best money fund managers and appears in each issue of *Barron's.*

Generally the average maturity of money market funds ranges from 30 to 50 days. When money fund managers expect interest rates to rise, they shorten the average maturity of the fund (reduce the number of days until the average investment in the portfolio matures). Donoghue calls it a danger signal when the average maturity of all taxable money funds is 39 days or less. In this case, investors should delay buying corporate bonds. However, if the average maturity is 46 days or longer and the average maturity has not declined during the past three weeks, money fund managers believe that interest rates are stable or falling. Consider buying corporate bonds at this time.

2. *Price of Gold.* Gold has been a sensitive barometer of the outlook for inflation. When investors are concerned about inflation, they buy gold. The increased demand pushes up gold prices. Rising inflation is usually accompanied by higher interest rates.

Declining gold prices reflect investors' confidence in the stability of future prices. Stable prices imply stable or declining interest rate levels.

3. *Prime Rate.* This is the rate charged by commercial banks to their most creditworthy business customers. This indicator is easy to follow since it is published daily in many newspapers, and changes in it

are also widely published. A decline in the prime rate generally follows a downturn in other short-term interest rates and indicates that bankers expect the trend to continue.

Tips. The following suggestions should be helpful to investors when purchasing corporate bonds:

- Limit your purchases of bonds to those listed on an exchange. Most bonds trade over-the-counter (OTC). However, many OTC bonds require you to pay your broker large spreads—the difference between the bid price and the asked price.
- Read the prospectus for information on vital matters such as call features (discussed in Key 15).
- Place a "limit" order when trading bonds. A limit order means the trade can be executed only at a specific price. Most bonds are seldom traded. The purchase or sale of just 5 to 10 bonds can change prices by several points. Target the highest price at which you will buy or the lowest price at which you will sell.
- Do not be misled by the bond's current yield. The issuer's creditworthiness and the bond's maturity are more important.
- Diversify. A portfolio should have a minimum of 10 to 15 bonds, although 20 to 25 is preferable. Buy bonds in different industries and diversify maturities.

Corporate bonds can also fill the need for those investors who seek a portfolio that will provide them with a regular monthly income. They should purchase desirable bonds that have the added feature of paying interest at different times, so that all the interest does not arrive in June and December. Standard & Poor's *Bond Guide* (1-212-208-8000 or your local library) lists the months when various corporations pay interest. The *Bond Guide* lists interest payment dates using the first letter ("m" indicates May) of each payment month. Since most bonds pay interest semiannually, two different months are listed with the letter for the month in which the bond matures being capitalized.

A final tip investors should consider. If you can't spend the time or lack the capital to observe these suggestions, consider buying a mutual fund that provides the dual advantages of diversification and professional management. A fund that provides solid performance at low cost is the Vanguard Bond Market Fund (1-800-62-7447). This fund is an index fund. Its objective is to duplicate the total return of the Salomon Brothers broad investment-grade bond index. This fund earned a return of 13.7% in 1989, almost 2% more than the total return for the average intermediate-term, investment-grade bond fund. Because the mechanical nature of bond indexing makes it unnecessary to have teams of highly paid analysts and investment strategists, costs are significantly lower than with actively managed bond investments. Vanguard's costs of operating its indexed bond fund in 1989 amounted to 0.32% of fund assets, or about one-third of the typical actively managed fund.

42

COMPOUNDING

The English economist John Maynard Keynes referred to compound interest as "magic." Compound interest is interest on interest and compounds when it remains in the account, becoming part of the principal that earns further interest. The magic in compounding is the tremendous rate at which savings can mount over the years. The following table shows how $10,000 invested in corporate bonds providing 10% interest paid semiannually can more than quadruple in value in only 15 years.

Compound Interest on a 10% $10,000 Investment

Time	Semiannual Interest	Cumulative Growth
6 months	$500	$10,500
1 year	525	11,025
1½ years	551	11,576
2 years	579	12,155
2½ years	608	12,763
3 years	638	13,401
3½ years	670	14,071
4 years	704	14,775

4½ years	739	15,514
5 years	776	16,290
5½ years	815	17,105
6 years	855	17,960
6½ years	898	18,858
7 years	943	19,801
7½ years	990	20,791
8 years	1,040	21,831
8½ years	1,092	22,923
9 years	1,146	24,069
9½ years	1,193	25,272
10 years	1,264	26,536
10½ years	1,324	27,860
11 years	1,393	29,253
11½ years	1,462	30,715
12 years	1,536	32,251
12½ years	1,613	33,864
13 years	1,693	35,557
13½ years	1,778	37,335
14 years	1,866	39,201
14½ years	1,960	41,161
15 years	2,058	43,219

Bondholders should realize the importance of reinvesting interest. If a person buys a bond and does not reinvest the interest received, then the principal remains constant. In the previous example, if the interest is not reinvested, the interest each period is based on the $10,000 rather than on the $10,000 plus the accumulated interest. Interest on $10,000 for 15 years at 10% payable semiannually accumulates to only $15,000 if not reinvested. In other words, the $10,000 original investment would total $25,000 ($10,000 + $15,000 interest) at the end of 15 years. The effect of compounding adds $18,219 ($43,219 – $25,000) to the total.

Interest does not have to be reinvested in the same bond. If better investment opportunities are available as interest payments are received, take advantage of them. It is important to remember that compounding works for you only if interest or dividends are reinvested. The simplest way to reinvest your returns is to purchase shares of a bond mutual fund that provides automatic reinvestment of interest earned.

Retirement Accounts. Corporate bonds make very good investments for IRAs or other retirement accounts. These investments provide more interest than government bonds, CDs, or money market accounts. Since the interest is tax free until retirement, higher-yielding corporate bonds make more sense than municipal or other tax-free investments in these accounts, which provide lower interest rates.

Bonds purchased for retirement accounts should have bond ratings of at least "A." The bonds selected should be the highest yielding bonds available with satisfactory financial conditions. You should choose new or recently issued bonds that cannot be called for at least 5 to 10 years. If you acquire a bond at a good interest rate, hold it until it matures. Investors should not actively buy or sell in retirement accounts. The most prudent form of bond investment for retirees probably is mutual funds. Some recommended selections include:

Vanguard Bond Market	(1-800-662-7447)
Vanguard Fixed Income- Investment Grade	(1-800-662-7447)
Bond Fund of America	(1-800-421-0180)
Axe-Houghton Income	(1-800-366-0444)

43

EVENT RISK

In 1988 RJR Nabisco was purchased by the leveraged buyout (LBO) firm of Kohlberg Kravis Roberts & Co. (KKR) for $14.7 billion. This purchase was financed by only $1.5 billion in equity. The remainder consisted of bond debt, bridge loans, preferred stock, junk bonds, and convertible debentures. The average price of RJR Nabisco's $5 billion of investment-grade bonds plummeted 20% in one week in October of 1988. The projected massive new debt transferred its investment-grade bonds into high-yield, high-risk junk bonds. The fear of the impact of LBOs affected the entire corporate bond market, raising yields on industrial bonds relative to other corporate issues.

The leveraged buyouts and mergers in the late 1980s added "event risk" to the bondholder's lexicon. Event risk was defined by Paul Ross, a managing director at Salomon Brothers, as "an occurrence not related to the fundamental credit quality of the issues and that an informed analyst could not reasonably have predicted." A surprise takeover proposal from a raider would be an example.

Event risk inflicted billions of dollars of losses on corporate bondholders between 1986 and 1989. A Salomon Brothers survey concluded that corporate bonds totaling $54 billion (out of $147 billion of bonds considered vulnerable) were affected by event risk, causing direct losses to investors of nearly $3 billion between 1986 and 1989.

Bondholders were so outraged by this development that they forced corporations to include covenant wording to protect their investments. These covenants, known as "poison puts," allow investors to get back their principal, and sometimes slightly more. They are usually triggered if a large percentage of a company's stock is purchased by a single buyer and the bond ratings are subsequently downgraded. For example, Federal Express included a poison put in its $100 million bond issuance of April 18, 1989, requiring that bondholders get their principal back if 30% of the stock is bought by a sole investor and ratings are then downgraded. A new type of poison put was structured by Bear, Stearns & Co. to enhance the salability of bonds by Enron Corp., a natural gas company. Enron's bonds are rated just above investment grade at BBB –. If the ratings drop one class, the 9.5% coupon rate jumps to 12%. If the ratings increase to A –, the rate eases to 9.4%.

By 1990 the cooling of the takeover mania had dampened event risk. Event risk activity sharply declined in late 1989 and the lessening of this risk continued in 1990. Although event risk may not be dead, it appears that it will be less of a factor in the 1990s.

Investors should not avoid the corporate bond market because of what happened to the bondholders of RJR Nabisco. They should, however, continue to exercise some caution. A well-diversified portfolio (a minimum of 10 to 15 bonds) or a mutual fund should minimize event risk. More bonds will become available that will include strict covenant wording. To avoid event risk altogether, buy bonds of utilities and finance companies that are relatively immune to takeover or restructuring activity.

44

DIVERSIFICATION

One of the keys to investment success is diversification. By investing in securities that do not move in tandem, investors can substantially reduce the fluctuation in the total return of their portfolio with little reduction in total return. However, diversification does not just mean acquiring a large number of securities. An investor could have held 100 different junk bonds recently and still have been ravaged by the events that affected this entire sector.

The basic strategy is to always have at least some investments that perform well to offset other investments that may be doing poorly. Diversification is helpful in reducing risk whenever you have securities with returns that are less than 100% correlated. In effect, it insures that at least part of the investor's portfolio will be invested in markets that are doing well.

Asset allocation applies diversification to different classes of investments. Investors can spread their portfolio among different types of assets such as stocks, bonds, international investments, and cash equivalents. Moreover, diversification within each of these classes is equally important. The key point is that diversification requires that portfolios contain securities with different patterns of returns.

The returns of U.S. stocks and bonds tend to be highly correlated about half the time because they react similarly to many of the same influences affecting the U.S. economy. However, the patterns of their returns are not highly correlated the other half of the time, which means they complement one another in a portfolio. Stocks offer superior growth potential when compared to bonds and have been a better hedge against inflation although both stock and bonds thrive when inflation is at moderate levels and suffer when inflation accelerates. In contrast, bonds provide higher current income and more stable returns than stocks.

Investors should remember that the value of U.S stocks is only about a third of the world total, while U.S. bonds represent about half of the world total. Foreign stocks and bonds can further diversify a portfolio because they are not highly correlated to U.S. economic risk and the U.S. dollar. They also allow investors to take advantage of profit opportunities internationally.

Diversification in Bonds. Most investors view diversification in terms of bonds as choosing the degree of default risk they are willing to assume. U.S. government bonds offer no default risk. Corporate bonds are subject to default but offer higher returns. High-yield or junk bonds have higher default risk but provide greater returns. And municipal bonds offer some default risk but provide tax sheltering of income.

The concept of diversification can be extended even further in the bond market. The primary risk investors face when purchasing bonds is interest rate risk. Bond prices are closely linked to the level of interest rates. As interest rates rise, bond prices fall; and as interest rates drop, bond prices rise.

However, not all sectors in the bond market fluctuate similarly in response to changes in interest rates. U.S. government bonds, investment-grade corporate bonds, and municipal bonds react in the same manner to changes in interest rates. However, two sectors of the bond market—high-yield bonds and international bonds—are affected by different variables and their price changes are not highly correlated to the price changes of U.S. government bonds, municipal bonds, and investment-grade bonds.

High-yield or junk bonds (ranked below BBB or Baa) are responsive not only to interest rates but also to the level of economic growth. Unlike investment-grade bonds, lower interest rates will not necessarily mean higher bond prices. Interest rates are less important than the performance of the economy in determining junk bond prices. Junk bonds are often issued by companies whose financial conditions are weak. Their balance sheet is loaded with debt. It is their ability to generate cash flows that will determine whether their obligation can be satisfied.

When the economy is robust, junk bonds tend to outperform other bonds. However, when the economy slows, junk bonds can plummet. An economic downturn depresses corporate earnings, making it difficult for highly leveraged companies to meet their debt obligations. Junk bonds are more akin to common stock than to investment-grade bonds in that they respond more to changes in corporate earnings and cash flow than to changes in interest rates.

International bonds also provide an opportunity to further diversify. An investment in a foreign bond can lead to a profit or loss in two ways:

1. The price of the bond in its local currency can advance or decline.

2. The value of the foreign currency may rise or fall relative to the U.S. dollar.

Studies have shown a low correlation between movements of bonds in the U.S. bond market and foreign markets.

The patterns of returns from U.S junk bonds and international bonds imply that investors can benefit by diversifying into these two sectors. In addition to smoothing out the volatily of bond prices, these sectors offer the possibility of higher returns. However, both of these areas require specialized knowledge that most investors lack. Interested investors should consider purchasing no-load mutual funds.

Junk bond mutual funds are discussed in Key 22. Two recommended international bond funds are:

Fidelity Global Fund   (1-800-544-6666)
T. Rowe Price International Bond (1-800-638-5660)

QUESTIONS AND ANSWERS

How difficult is it to time the bond market?

It is indeed very difficult to predict future movements of prices in the bond market. A study publi-
cized in 1990 by the Hulbert Financial Digest of
Alexandria, Virginia reveals that only one newsletter
out of 18 beat the Shearson Lehman Treasury Bond
index during 1989. In addition, none of the five letters
monitored by Hulbert from 1985 through 1989 came
close to matching the index over the same period.

It may be more difficult for investors to reap
abnormal return in bonds than in stocks. The bond
markets are more dominated by professional investors than the stock markets, so it becomes even less
likely that the average investor will outperform the
market.

What strategy should an individual investor follow?

One approach recommended by some professionals
is to buy bonds with widely varying maturities. This
strategy, referred to as "laddering," is a form of
diversification. Another approach is to invest in index
funds, which simply attempt to mimic the performance of a widely followed market index. An example
is the Vanguard Bond Market Fund (1-800-662-7447),
which attempts to duplicate the Salomon Brothers
broad investment-grade bond index.

This book discusses various timing techniques in
Keys 41 and 13, entitled "Buying Corporate Bonds"
and "Timing Bond Purchases." Those investors seek-
ing a newsletter for advice can subscribe to Systems
and Forecasts (1-516-829-6444), ranked first in per-

formance for the five-year period 1985 to 1989 by Hulbert Financial Digest.

Should I use a discount broker?

If you don't seek or want advice, you should consider using discount brokers. The biggest advantage is the lower commission costs. Customers of discount brokers can expect to pay about half the commission charged by a full-service broker. Discount brokers are able to offer these lower rates because they do not provide research. Salaried order clerks handle the transactions rather than commissioned brokers, and they maintain low overhead.

Discount brokers work on salary rather than on commission. Their purpose is to execute transactions, not persuade you to invest by making a sales pitch. Their income is not dependent upon the number of trades investors make. Like full-service brokers, discount firms will send investors confirmations of orders and monthly statements and will safeguard their certificates if desired.

What are redemption fees and 12b-1 plans?

Until recently, mutual funds were either load or no-load. But today, fee structures are more complex and confusing to investors. Among these fees are redemption fees, also called contingent deferred sales charges or back-end loads. This fee is charged when investors sell their shares, usually within a fixed period. It may be a flat percentage of the sales price or may by based on a sliding scale, say 5% the first year, declining in steps to 0% in year 5.

Under the controversial 12b-1 plans, the fund can charge a fee to pay for its marketing and promotion costs. A 12b-1 fee can be levied on the full value of the investment each year or on the original value of the investment. Any such fee over 1% is excessive.

All funds also charge a management fee in order to compensate the asset managers for their services. These fees range from around 0.3% of the funds' assets to 2% or even more.

Information on fees and other expense data is available on page 2 of every mutual fund prospectus. Investors should always read this page before purchasing a mutual fund.

Investors do not always get what they pay for. Thus, the funds that charge the highest fees do not necessarily increase in value faster than the "cheaper" funds.

What is the difference between yield and total return?

Yield is the percentage return on an investor's money in terms of current prices. For bonds, it is the annual interest per bond divided by the current market price. A bond that provides interest of $96 per year and sells for 120 ($1200 per bond) yields 8%.

Total return is yield plus or minus capital gains and losses. Investors should always be primarily concerned with total return and not yield. Even if a fund has an excellent yield, its return can be terrible if its principal declines. Although junk bonds had yields of 12 to 20% in 1989, their total return dropped 4% in 1989 because of declining prices.

Investors should be wary of investments promising extraordinary yields. Ask for the prospectus to get the true picture. SEC rules require disclosure of historical total returns in the prospectus.

How good an investment are corporate bonds compared to other securities?

Many investors are disillusioned with corporate bonds because of their experience in the 1960s and 1970s when corporate bonds were actually earning negative returns (total returns were less than the rate of inflation). However, this is a case where history may be misleading. Granted, corporate bonds have often been a poor investment in the past. Nevertheless, investors who ignore this market are missing out on generous returns. Currently, in order to sell bonds, corporations have to price them to compensate investors for the inflation outlook, the greater instability of interest rates today, and the consequent increased volatility of bond prices. Bond prices no longer yield 5% or less coupon interest. Instead, high quality corporate bonds now yield 9.5% interest. This return compares favorably with the average 10% return from common stock. Investors should remember that stocks are still more risky than bonds, and there have been extended periods, such as the years 1966 to 1982, when it was difficult to make money trading stocks.

In conclusion, if investors want to protect their principal and receive a steady stream of income, bonds rather than stocks may be the answer. Interest from corporate bonds will exceed the income to be received from CDs, government bonds, money market funds, and stocks. Corporate bonds are appropriate for every portfolio, and bonds are particularly appropriate for the tax-protected retirement plans where interest can compound free of tax.

Should I invest in junk bonds?

Junk bonds are corporate bonds rated below BBB or Baa by the ratings agencies. The junk bond market has been battered recently by the indictment of Michael Milken and the bankruptcies of several major firms issuing junk bonds. This sector is further troubled by the lack of secondary liquidity and the difficulty of pricing many securities that are infrequently traded.

Although the average junk bond return of over 16% in early 1990 is very attractive, investors should be cautious about this market. The default rate is increasing and for many of these financially shaky companies the consequences of a recession would be serious. Junk bonds should be only a small part of any investor's portfolio, and diversification is absolutely necessary to reduce risk to acceptable levels.

What is the most important factor affecting the price of investment-grade (at least BBB or Baa) bonds?

The price of a bond is determined by the interest rate stated on the bond, the length of its term to maturity, and the prevailing market interest rate or yield on the bond. Bonds fluctuate in price primarily as a result of a change in the general level of interest rates. As interest rates rise, bond prices go down; as interest rates fall, bond prices increase. The course of bond prices is largely dependent upon the path of interest rates.

The intimate relationship of interest rates to bond prices explains why market timing, when applied to bonds, is primarily a matter of anticipating interest rate changes. However, interest rates respond to many factors, and this makes forecasting their changes very difficult if not impossible for the average investor. Market timing becomes less important if the investor has an effectively diversified portfolio.

How does the Securities and Exchange Commission (SEC) serve the investor?

The SEC was established by Congress to administer federal laws that seek to provide protection for investors. The overriding purpose of these laws is to ensure the integrity of the securities markets by requiring full disclosure of material facts related to securities offered to the public for sale.

The SEC does not insure investors. Nor does it prevent the sale of securities in risky, poorly managed, or unprofitable companies. Rather, registration with the SEC is designed to provide adequate and accurate disclosure of required material facts about the company and the securities it proposes to sell. A portion of the information included in the registration statement is included in a prospectus that is prepared for public distribution.

The SEC requires the continual disclosure of company information through annual, quarterly, and special reports. Form 10-K is the annual report that contains a myriad of financial data in addition to nonfinancial information, such as the name of corporate officers and directors and the extent of their ownership. Form 10-Q is the quarterly report that contains abbreviated financial and nonfinancial information. Form 8-K is a report of material events or corporate changes deemed to be of importance to the shareholders or the SEC. All of these can be obtained from the company or the SEC.

What is the efficient market hypothesis (EMH)?

Although the EMH has been a topic of academic interest and debate for the past 25 years, it has only recently received the attention of the financial press. Market efficiency is a description of how prices in competitive markets react to new information. An efficient market is one in which prices adjust rapidly to new information and in which current prices fully reflect all available information. The adjustments in stock or bond prices occur so rapidly that an investor cannot use publicly available information to earn above-average profits.

Although many analysts are dubious about the EMH, it does provide some important lessons that should be absorbed by all investors:

    1. Tips are almost always of no value. The market processes new information very quickly.

    2. A portfolio should not be churned. A strategy that involves frequent purchases and sales of bonds is

likely to be a loser because the commission costs eat up any profits an investor might make.

3. It is not easy to beat the market. Only a small minority of investors can consistently outperform the market. High returns can usually be achieved only through assuming greater risk. However, greater risk raises the possibility of increased losses as well as gains.

What is the difference between technical analysis and fundamental analysis?

Technical analysis is the attempt to predict future bond price movements by analyzing the past sequence of bond prices. Technical analysts do not consider such factors as monetary and fiscal policies, political environment, industry trends, or company earnings and financial condition in predicting future bond prices. Their concern is with the historical movement of prices and the forces of supply and demand that affect prices. Technical analysis is frequently contrasted with fundamental analysis, which attempts to measure the intrinsic value of a security and places considerable reliance upon financial statements and economic trends.

Fundamental analysis is far less important to bondholders than to stockholders because of the widespread reliance on bond rating agenies of in-depth analysis of the risk of default. Most bond investors rely on the ratings agencies to determine the default risk of a bond. Other information required by bond investors is information on market and economic conditions and on intrinsic bond features. Key 30, entitled "Sources of Information," provides specific references.

GLOSSARY

Arbitrage profiting from differences in price when the same security is traded on two or more markets.

Asked Price price at which dealers are willing to sell a security.

Asset economic resources expected to provide future benefits to a firm.

Balance Sheet financial statement showing a firm's assets, liabilities, and stockholders' equity as of a particular date.

Bear Market prolonged period of declining prices of securities.

Bid Price price at which dealers are willing to purchase a security.

Bond Indenture contract between an issuer of bonds and the bondholder, which includes provisions such as the form of bond, amount of issue, property pledged (if any), protective covenants, and working capital requirements.

Bond Rating system of evaluating the credit quality of bonds by assigning the bonds to different risk classifications.

Bond Swap simultaneous sale of one bond issue and purchase of another.

Bull Market prolonged period of rising prices of securities.

Callable Bond bond redeemable by the issuer before its maturity date.

Closed-end Mutual Fund a fund that offers a fixed number of shares that are traded on exchanges like stocks and bonds.

Common Stock ownership of a public corporation represented by shares of stock.

Consumer Price Index change in consumer prices determined by a monthly survey of the U.S. Bureau of

Labor Statistics.

Convertible Bond   bond that can be exchanged into a specified amount of common stock at a specified price.

Corporate Bond   debt instrument issued by a private corporation.

Coupon Rate   specified rate of interest that a corporation will pay the bondholders expressed as an annual percentage of face value.

Current Yield   annual interest on a bond divided by its current market price.

Debenture   general debt obligation not secured by any assets of the borrower.

Dividends   payment made by a corporation to its stockholders.

Face Value (par value, maturity value)   amount the corporation must repay on the maturity date.

Federal Reserve System   central bank of the United States, which formulates monetary policy and controls the money supply.

Gross National Product   measurement of economic activity by computing the total market value of all goods and services produced in a given period.

Income Statement   financial statement that discloses a firm's revenues and expenses over a period of time.

Inflation Rate   rate of change in the prices of goods and services.

Interest Rate   rate charged for the use of money.

Investment Grade   term used to describe bonds with a bond rating of BBB (Baa) or better.

Junk Bond   a high-risk, high-yield bond (lower than BBB or Baa bond rating).

Leveraged Buyout   process of buying a corporation's stock with borrowed money, then repaying the debt from the corporation's assets.

Limit Orders   order to buy or sell a security at a specific price or better.

Liquidity the ease with which an asset can be converted into cash, reflecting a firm's ability to meet its short-term obligations.

Load Funds type of mutual fund where the buyer must pay a sales fee, or commission, on top of the price.

Margin amount a customer deposits with a broker when borrowing from the broker to buy securities.

Market Orders order to buy or sell a security at the best available price.

Monetary Policy actions by the Federal Reserve to control the money supply, bank lending, and the interest rates.

Money Supply sum total of money in an economy, primarily including currency held by the public plus transations accounts in depository institutions and traveler's checks.

Municipal Bond tax-exempt security issued by state and local government agencies and authorities.

Mutual Fund pool of commingled funds contributed by investors and managed by professional managers for a fee.

NASDAQ National Association of Securities Dealers Automated Quotations; a computerized communications network that provides automated quotations (bid and asked prices) on stocks and bonds.

No-Load Fund type of mutual fund for which no commission is charged to make a purchase.

Open-End Bond Fund fund that issues more shares as investors purchase more shares at a price equal to net asset value.

Option right to buy or sell property that is granted in exchange for an agreed-upon sum.

Over-The-Counter trades securities through a centralized computer telephone network that links dealers across the U.S.

Poison Puts covenant that protects investors in the

event of takeover by requiring that the exisiting bonds be retired at par value or slightly above par value.

Preferred Stock   class of stock that has certain preferential rights over common stock.

Prime Rate   interest rate charged by banks to their most creditworthy business customers.

Prospectus   formal wirtten offer to sell securities; includes audited financial statements and other information about the company.

Real Interest Rate   nominal rate of interest less the anticipated rate of inflation.

Securities and Exchange Commission   U.S. government agency that administers the federal laws that protect the investor.

Senior Issue   security that has a claim prior to a more recent obligation on a corporation's assets and earnings.

Shareholders   the owners of a corporation.

Sinking Fund   money accumulated on a regular basis that is used to redeem debt securities.

Subordinated Bond   bond that is junior to older securities or debts in its claim on assets.

Tombstone Announcement   advertisement by investment bankers of a public offering of securites, giving basic details about the issue.

Treasury Bill Rate   the interest rate on short-term government securities that are issued in minimum denominations of $10,000 with $5,000 increments.

Treasury Issues   debt obligations of the U.S. government, secured by its full faith and credit. The income from treasuries is exempt from state and local but not federal taxes.

Warrants   options to buy a specified number of common shares at a predetermined price within a fixed time period.

Yield to Maturity   concept used to determine the rate of return an investor will receive if a bond is held to its maturity date. It includes both interest and the appreciation to face value at maturity when the bonds are bought at a discount or depreciation to face value when the bonds are bought at a premium.

Zero-Coupon Bond a bond that does not make periodic interest payments but instead is sold at a deep discount from its face value.

INDEX